Femininity is a source of shame for some men and women. Scholarship and therapeutic practice have not reckoned with femininity of its shamefulness in helpful, healing ways. Thus, women and men continue to hide their "feminine" selves. This book asserts the positive worth and power of femininity for men and women; men's and women's need for validation of their femininity; and the need to create child-rearing and therapeutic practices that achieve incorporation of femininity in men's conscious self-understanding.

Author Biography: Barbara L. Eurich-Rascoe is Adjunct Professor and Director of the Office of Women's Concerns at Fuller Theological Seminary in Pasadena, California. Hendrika Vande Kemp is Professor of Psychology at Fuller Theological Seminary.

FEMININITY AND SHAME

Women, Men, and Giving Voice to the Feminine

Barbara L. Eurich-Rascoe
Hendrika Vande Kemp

University Press of America, Inc.
Lanham • New York • Oxford

Copyright © 1997 by
University Press of America,® Inc.
4720 Boston Way
Lanham, Maryland 20706

12 Hid's Copse Rd.
Cummor Hill, Oxford OX2 9JJ

All rights reserved
Printed in the United States of America
British Library Cataloguing in Publication Information Available

Library of Congress Cataloging-in-Publication Data

Eurich-Rascoe, Barbara L.
Femininity and shame : women, men, and giving voice to the feminine / Barbara L. Eurich-Rascoe, Hendrika Vande Kemp.
p. cm.
Includes bibliographical references and index.
1. Women--Identity. 2. Women--Socialization. 3. Identity (Psychology) 4. Femininity (Psychology) 5. Shame. I. Vande Kemp, Hendrika. II. Title.
HQ1206.E93 1997 155.6'33--dc21 96-52829 CIP

ISBN 0-7618-0677-6(cloth: alk. ppr.)
ISBN 0-7618-0678-4 (pbk: alk. ppr.)

∞™ The paper used in this publication meets the minimum requirements of American National Standard for information Sciences—Permanence of Paper for Printed Library Materials, ANSI Z39.48—1984

Acknowledgments

With gratitude to so many friends and family members without whose assistance this project would never have been completed.

Structural Analysis of Social Behavior, Model, Cluster Version. In "Use of the SASB dimensional model to develop treatment plans for personality disorders. I: Narcissism," by Lorna Smith Benjamin, *Journal of Personality Disorders, 1*, 43–70. Copyright 1987. Used by permission of Guilford Press.

Table of Contents

Acknowledgments	iii
List of Tables	ix
List of Figures	xi

Introduction. Women and Voicelessness	1
Chapter 1. Identity and Voice	9
The Self-in-Relation	10
Conceptions of the Self	11
Erikson and Ego Identity	12
Hartmann and the Adaptive Ego	14
Jung and the Gendered Ego	16
Critiques of the Concept of the Bounded, Masterful Self	17
Together and Apart: Building a Case for Wholeness	19
Adolescence: Time to Separate or Connect	19
Beginning with Connection	21
Voice, Language, and Identity Formation	23
Language and Speech	23
The Wordless Voice	25
Conclusion	25

Chapter 2. Gender: Feminine and Masculine Defined	29
Gender and Sex	30
Sex	31
Gender	33
Summary	42
Gender and the Structural Analysis of Social Behavior	43
Identifying Gender Using the Structural Analysis of Social Behavior	47
Conclusion: Values and Gender	52
Chapter 3. A Brief History of Sex and Gender	55
Early Philosophy, Theology, and Biological Determinism	55
Gnosticism	56
The Renaissance and the Enlightenment	57
Freud and Freudians	60
Challenges to Freud	61
Adler, Ferenczi, and Rank	62
Jung and gender	63
Post-Jungians and gender	64
Cultural Anthropology and Sociology	65
Erikson and Kohlberg	66
Late Twentieth-Century Feminism	67
Sandra Bem and Androgyny	68
Identity Development and Sex Difference	69
Sex and Gender Difference	70
Relatedness and Psychoanalytic Thought	73
Conclusion	75
Chapter 4. Shame and Femininity	77
Shame and Gender	77
Women and Femininity	78
Men and Femininity	79
Masculinity and Shame	83
Shame	85

Shame and Interpersonal Relatedness 88
   Shame, Sex, and Pride 90
   Sex, Gender, and Envy 92
The Evocation of Shame 92
Identifying the Interpersonal Sequences of
the Shame Event 93
   Punishment 94
   Mystification 95
   Double-bind 98
   Projective Identification 98
   Voicelessness and Violence 99
Conclusion 99

Chapter 5. Power and Gender 103
Power and the Structural Analysis
of Social Behavior 105
   Dominant Power and Codetermined Power 106
   Use and Abuse of Power 108
   Feminine Power and Masculine Power 110
Power, Gender and the Family 112
Power, Gender, and the Practice of Psychotherapy 115
Conclusion 119

Chapter 6. Conclusion 121

Epilogue. Sustenance Culture Tales 133

Notes 135

References 149

Index 171

List of Tables

Table 1. Gender Identification and Expression 31

Table 2. Contributing Factors to Current Popular
Understandings of Feminine and Masculine 32

Table 3. Masculine and Feminine Descriptors
From the Bem Sex Role Inventory 38

Table 4. Comparison BSRI Gender Items
and SASB Social Behaviors: Feminine Descriptors 48

Table 5. Comparison BSRI Gender Items
and SASB Social Behaviors: Masculine Descriptors 49

List of Figures

Figure 1. Variables which are confounded in operational definitions of gender: (a) traditional definition; (b) current definition of gender as "men" or "women" as social groups; (c) unconfounded definition of gender as a personality variable.   35

Figure 2. Cluster version of the SASB Model. From "Use of the SASB dimensional model to develop treatment plans for personality disorders. I: Narcissism," L. S. Benjamin, 1987a, *Journal of Personality Disorders, 1*, 43–70. Copyright, 1987, The Guilford Press. Reprinted with permission.   44

Figure 3. Cluster version of the SASB Model, with masculine and feminine social behaviors designated.   51

Introduction.
Women and Voicelessness

"He was oppressed, and he was afflicted, yet he opened not his mouth: he is brought as a lamb to the slaughter, and as a sheep before her shearers is dumb, so he openeth not his mouth."

Isaiah 53:7 (KJV)

The problem of women's voicelessness has a long history in western culture (Sampson, 1993).[1] *Voice*, as a metaphor for freedom, power, assertiveness and self-determination, has often been denied to women. These traits have been viewed as the prerogatives of men. Until recently women were perceived as incompetent to rule themselves or their families. Two waves of a social movement for expanding women's rights (a form of voice) in the United States and other North American and western European countries have assisted women in gaining the rights to vote; to hold property, and to obtain education and jobs which were once available only to men. Female voices are being heard increasingly on public affairs as they become more involved in the academy, the marketplace, and the political arena.

In the last five years the problem of women's voicelessness has resurfaced in a variety of popular culture contexts,[2] as in the cinema and the theater, with such stories as *The Phantom of the Opera* (Webber & Hart, 1987), *The Little Mermaid* (Musker & Clements and Ashman & Musker, 1990), *Beauty and the Beast* (Tronsdale & Wise and Hahn, 1991), and *The Piano* (Campion & Chapman, 1994). In these tales, as well as in nonfiction, the themes of woman's voice and voicelessness have come into sharper focus.

The metaphors of having a voice and losing one's voice are dominant themes in the Disney Productions interpretation of the Hans Christian Anderson (1942/1989) fairy tale, *The Little Mermaid,* and in the music of Andrew Lloyd Webber's version of the Leroux (1911) novel, *The Phantom of the Opera*. In each piece of fiction, the ending portrays a young woman with a remarkable singing voice drifting off into the sunset with a handsome prince and renouncing the public use of her beautiful voice. These two tales describe the experiences of two late adolescent women who are attempting both to identify and develop their creative potentials and to restrict themselves to conventional sex roles in conventional social settings. Many features of these two stories create tensions that are not resolved by their conclusions: the role of the community in silencing the woman's voices; the role of aggression in silencing her voice; the source of the man's need for the woman's voicelessness; the woman's willingness to sacrifice her voice in order to relate to her lover.

In the Disney Productions version of the de Beaumont *Beauty and the Beast* (1780/1992) folktale a very different story emerges. As in *Phantom* and *Mermaid*, an adolescent girl who has no mother is attempting to find her own place in life; she, too, has a doting father who is emotionally unavailable to her; and she meets and falls in love with a man who is transformed by her love and whom she eventually marries. However, rather than having a singing voice, this young woman has her own ideas and her own desire for adventures; she has strong opinions which she expresses freely and naively; her community finds her odd but does not press her to conform. The growth and development of her character depends on the continuing use of her speaking voice in rejecting the conventions that would restrict her, in rejecting the advances of a conventional man, in serving her father's need, in serving her lover's need, and in describing her own desires.

The film *The Piano* (Campion & Chapman, 1994) portrays an even different tale of voice and voicelessness. A young girl loses her voice in a way that is not clear, but finds self-expression in playing the piano. She is not her own, nor is her piano hers. The movie chronicles her journey from being the silenced property of her family and, then, of her husband, to becoming the free partner of a man who can hear and celebrate and participate in her expression of herself and her passion. At the end of the film, she is teaching and playing piano, and, more importantly, learning to speak.

The popularity of these tales suggests that contemporary realities are being reflected in these fictional works. These metaphors of "voice" stir recognition in women: Women see in these tales a reflection of their own lives and development. What is it in women's lives these storytellers are attempting to describe with metaphors of voice and voicelessness?

Introduction

In Carol Gilligan's (1982) *In A Different Voice*, the term "voice" is used to designate self-expression, personal power, and moral force. She reflected on women's unique capacities to express relational power in society because of unique features of their moral reasoning. She used the term "voice" such that it also represents differences between the ways young men and young women reason in making moral and ethical decisions. She discovered in her research that men and women use different criteria; women as a group tend to argue for their moral decisions based on what Gilligan called an "ethic of care" or "responsibility ethic," while men as a group tend to use an "ethic of rights." Gilligan developed a description of the ethic of care, the woman's way, giving a distinctive meaning to her metaphor of "voice."

Since the publication of *In A Different Voice* (Gilligan, 1982), other psychologists researching women have taken up the metaphor of voice in attempting to portray accurately other aspects of women's experience. Belenky, Clinchy, Goldberger, and Tarule (1986), following Gilligan's lead, suggested that woman's epistemology develops differently from men's due to women's different learning experiences and learning environments. They suggested that women are "constructive knowers."[3] While men have often been portrayed as objective knowers (Sampson, 1978), Perry (1970) described a developmental process in men that led to an epistemological position of relativism, and a recognition that truth is "constructed." Perry's work was used as a foundation by Belenky et al. (1986) to explicitly challenge cultural appraisals of women's moral and rational processes, a challenge that is designed to assert the validity of women's experience. Belenky and her colleagues found that

> women's perspectives on knowing [can be grouped] into five ... categories: *silence,* a position in which women experience themselves as mindless and voiceless and subject to the whims of external authority; *received knowledge,* a perspective from which women conceive of themselves as capable of receiving, even reproducing, knowledge from the all-knowing external authorities; *subjective knowledge,* a perspective from which truth and knowledge are conceived of as personal, private, and subjectively known or intuited; *procedural knowledge,* a position in which women are invested in learning and applying objective procedures for obtaining and communicating knowledge; and *constructed knowledge,* a position in which women view all knowledge as contextual, experience themselves as creators of knowledge, and value both subjective and objective strategies for knowing. (p. 15)

In their model, womanly epistemology is described, using the language of the research participants, by metaphors of voice and hearing (in contrast to the metaphors of sight and seeing which are common in earlier models that used only male subjects).4 Belenky and her colleagues suggested that women have an experience of finding and losing or, in some cases, never having a voice and for women voice has to do with the power to describe their own lives and to effect their own changes (see also Gilligan, Lyons, & Hanmer, 1990; Gilligan, Ward, Taylor, & Bardige, 1988).

Gilligan (1982) used the term *voice* to designate: (a) The process[5] of women's argumentation as they reason, and (b) the particular contents of their experience which shape the arguments they use to justify their moral choices. She used voice to signify the capacity to declare one's methods and principles of moral decision-making; thus, as a process, voice might be described as a person's ability to declare, to stand in (or, to maintain), and to stand for one's own experience. She reported that women use different experiences and premises (i.e., different data) than men to inform and to make moral choices; as a particular content, voice is the expression of those particular differences and the particular results to which they give rise. A critical feature of Gilligan's work is that she identifies a difference in values of women as compared to men, as well as a difference in rational and emotional components of the process; women value closeness over distance and emotion as well as reason. Men as a group tend to suppress the emotions of the situation in order to arrive at "objective" truth, while women as a group tend to include emotion as an additional or an alternative category of information. It is this inclusion of emotion by women, especially of tenderness and the desire for affiliation, that has been evaluated as less mature and less healthy by earlier theorists (see Erikson, 1950, 1964, 1968; Freud, 1925, 1931; Kohlberg, 1958, 1973, 1981; Kohlberg & Kramer, 1969).

Voice, as a metaphor, is like *agency*, which is the capacity to exert power, and *autonomy*, which is self-governance or independence. It has some similarity to *identity*, which signifies the essential character, content and connections, as well as the limits and limitations, of one's own person; and to *mastery*, which indicates proficiency and competence in a behavioral realm.[6] *Mastery* and *agency* suggest behavioral and conative capacities, while identity and autonomy suggest interpersonal and intrapersonal capacities which are primarily cognitive and affective. *Voice* suggests a declaration of and an adherence to personal values in an interpersonal arena.[7] For example, to use Gilligan's focus on moral decision-making, it is conceivable that one could act alone out of a sense of moral right, but it is difficult to imagine a person acting without relationship to and involvement with other persons when using an ethic of care.[8] The metaphor *voice* suggests such concepts as agency, autonomy, identity, and mastery. However, as *voice* is used in current culture tales and in research on women's identity, its primary distinctive is *self-declaration in an interpersonal context that has the primary goal of maintaining interpersonal connection.* That is, voice declares, in an interpersonal context, both the reality and integrity of the self and the reality of the interpersonal connection while seeking to maintain and enhance that connection.

In the past it has been difficult to describe women's unique experiences accurately in ways that are free from the implicit negative valorization of women and their traditional roles that has been a subtext in the standard developmental theories of Freud, Erikson, Kohlberg, and others. The effort to include girls' and womens' different experiences is recent. Also, those researching men's development have been attempting to understand how boys and men are silenced in the expression of those "girlish," "womanish," or "feminine"[9] parts of their experience (Brod, 1987; Johnson, 1989a, 1989b, 1991; Kupers, 1993; Lynn, 1969; Monick, 1987, 1991; Mussen, Conger, & Kagan, 1969; Mussen & Dikstra, 1961; Pleck, 1981).

Have women, in fact, found a voice in the sense that it is being used here? Perhaps women have found a voice to the extent that they have gained access to some experience of what the dominant culture approves to be voiced, so the experience to which they give voice is an acceptable one. That is, women have become more involved in the academy, the factory, and the marketplace: the public sphere. They have learned *men's* language in *men's* arenas, and so can converse with men on *men's* terms. However, as stated by Csiksazentmihalyi (1989) in his review of Gilligan's *Mapping the Moral Domain*,

"One disturbing finding [is that] as girls become more involved in the institutional roles of the world of men ... their 'voices' change into masculine baritones. ... care and personal involvement [are replaced by] recourse to impersonal justice" (p. 6).

For example: A woman is expressing an idea to which she is passionately committed; the man with whom she is speaking fidgets uncomfortably and looks away; she takes a deep breath, and begins again, dispassionately; he relaxes and responds with relief, agreement and promises of support. Passion (in fact, any emotionality but anger) is not "manly," so it cannot be heard (Lerner, 1985). If a woman's particular experiences are expressed in or for her womanliness, the woman is likely to remain unheard. She is voiceless. What this silencing of womanliness highlights is that having a voice involves more than a speaker; a hearer, a responder, is also a necessary component to the experience of having a voice (Bernstein & Gilligan, 1990; Corbett, 1971; Gilligan, 1990; McCluhan, 1967). Women face a dilemma.[10] In the public domain a woman is expected to be assertive; however, assertiveness is a task labeled by the culture as "masculine" (Bem, 1974) and unwomanly. She is behaving in a way that is proscribed by traditional social roles, so her assertion, when expressed in its typical social context, is a form of communication that is both more difficult for her to express and more difficult for the hearer to hear. Further, if the content of her assertion is her experience of care and connection, of mutuality and reciprocity, then the content is labeled feminine and nonassertive, according to cultural definitions (Bem, 1974). By definition, the act of assertion is autonomous and often carries the connotation of aggression or disaffiliation ("assert," *Merriam-Webster's Collegiate Dictionary*, 1993), while the verbal content expresses affiliation and interdependence. Thus, in this case, the action of assertion attempts to communicate nonassertion as content. The communication becomes a contradiction that is both difficult to voice and to hear.[11]

While *voice* has become a common metaphor for women's free expression of personhood and of personal power, training and maintaining a strong female voice is not so common. According to Gilligan and her colleagues (Gilligan, 1982; Gilligan et al., 1988, 1990), girls face a serious crisis of potential silencing at adolescence when they begin to experience societal pressure to choose pursuits that subsume identity in relationship and home or those that delimit identity by independence and career. Like the heroines in the stories related at the beginning of the chapter, girls today find it difficult to keep their own voices and continue to speak.[12] Women, as well as girls, feel many pressures to choose one way or another (Wallis, 1989); much of the stress and fatigue being experienced currently by American middle-class women is a result of living the tension. Some culture critics (Limbaugh, 1992; Moir & Jessell, 1991) suggest that women are returning to home and hearth because they are biologically predisposed to tasks of childcare. However, their critiques may be predicated on ideological assumptions that does no accurately reflect the myriad expressions of complex human experience.

Voice is an important contemporary metaphor for women's attempts to add their unique characters and experiences to social discourse for the goal of achieving greater understanding of human nature. The purpose of this study is: (a) to describe the identity-voice connection in women (Chapter 1); (b) to establish that it is femininity in women and men that is silenced (Chapter 2); (c) to trace the denigration of the feminine

Introduction 7

through history (Chapter 3); (d) to establish the connection between historical trends of devaluation of the feminine and interpersonal communications that induce shame, specifically to identify social-behavioral messages that silence those expressing femininity (Chapter 4); and (e) to describe feminine power and masculine power, asserting the potential for their coexistence and cooperation, even within the individual, and suggesting how the function of the family and the practice of psychotherapy may help men and women reclaim valuable feminine parts of themselves that have been split off from awareness (Chapter 5).

The meaning of *voice* in this work will be *self-declaration in an interpersonal context that has the primary goal of maintaining interpersonal connection*. This definition does not imply the necessity of using opposition or aggression in the process of self-expression. *Voice* has power: power to communicate, to persuade, whether feminine or masculine. *Voice* expresses the self: its character, limits, and values; and its connection to other selves.

Chapter 1.
Identity and Voice

> "If there is no one in the forest when a tree falls, will its falling make a sound?"
> A classical conundrum

Voice is a current popular metaphor for the ability to express the subjective, individual experience of the self; it is related to the exercise of freedom and power. Through the work of Gilligan (1982) and Belenky et al. (1986), the metaphor of voice has come to be associated with the concepts of identity and the self. Many students of psychology, philosophy, religion, and spirituality have explored the concept of the self, and the closely related concept of identity. Surrey (1991) defines "self" as "a construct useful in describing the organization of a person's experience and [the] construction of reality that illuminates the purpose and directionality of her or his behavior" (p. 52). Current research suggests that women in western culture may have selves (or identities) that are different from the selves of men.

This chapter will describe: (a) The current concept of a self-in-relation, as presented by Jordan, Kaplan, Miller, Stiver, and Surrey (1991), a model of women's identity and its formation; (b) earlier conceptions of identity to which current theories of women's development are reacting; (c) current philosophical psychological critiques of the earlier concepts; (d) the convergence of various descriptions of the self and identity that arise from recent studies in adolescent development and object relations theory; and (e) current discussions of voice production and language acquisition that elucidate the identity-voice connection.

The Self-in-Relation

Jordan et al. (1991), building on the work of Jean Baker Miller (1976), have described a different self and development of self in women as compared to a standard that has been based on studies of men. They have named this woman's self the *self-in-relation* to distinguish it from the separate and autonomous self that has been dominant in earlier (male) models. According to Surrey (1991), observers often confuse the interdependence which characterizes women's relationships with dependence and symbiosis. The term *interdependence* here suggests a relationship between persons that is characterized by mutual care, trust, and reliance on the other(s) as well as by the capacity for independent action. *Dependency* connotes a relationship that is characterized by the fact that the well-being of one member is contingent on the care provided by the other member(s), but not the reverse. *Symbiosis*, when used to describe human relationship, usually refers to a state of union in which at least one member is relatively unaware of the other as an independent, instrumental being (Mahler, 1975).

Women have often been labeled as sick, weak, immature or immoral because they do not separate their selves from their significant others in the same way that men do (see Deutsch, 1945; Erikson, 1950, 1964, 1968; Freud, 1925, 1931; Horney, 1967; Kohlberg, 1958, 1973, 1981; Kohlberg & Kramer, 1969). This negative evaluation arises from the application of developmental schema that implicitly value the independent and separate self as the singular expression of healthy personhood (Broverman, Broverman, Clarkson, Rosenkratz, & Vogel, 1970; Broverman, Vogel, Broverman, Clarkson, & Rosenkratz, 1972; Cushman, 1990). By default, girls' and women's developmental experiences have been labeled abnormal because their selves are other-embedded.[1] Surrey (1991) contends that interdependence is a healthy outcome of women's self development.

Surrey (1991) describes the processes of development that lead to the formation of a woman's self-in-relation and defines the concept, self-in-relation. She states that women have a sense of self that can be described as:

(1) an interest in and attention to the other person(s), which form the base for the emotional connection and the ability to empathize with the other(s); (2) the expectation of a mutual empathic process where the sharing of experience leads to a heightened development of self and other; and (3) the expectation of interaction and relationship as a process of mutual sensitivity and mutual responsibility that provides

the stimulus for growth of empowerment and self-knowledge. (pp. 58–59)

In order to achieve the qualities of a self-in-relation as described above, a woman must grow up in an interpersonal environment that is fundamentally empathic. Following and synthesizing the work of Chodorow (1978), Kohut (1971), Miller (1976), and Winnicott (1971), Surrey (1991) states that the relationship with the mother provides an environment for the daughter that is different from that which she provides for the son. For the daughter the relationship with the mother fosters and gratifies her interest in an ongoing connection with the mother, while little boys may experience closeness with mother as "invasive, engulfing, or threatening" (p. 55). Second, the daughter learns how to mirror her mother accurately due to her mother's emotional openness and through her experience of being mirrored accurately by the mother, while for the son developmental processes emphasize separation and disidentification. Third, "emotional and cognitive connections based on shared understanding develop over time into a mutual process in which both mothers and daughters become highly responsive to the feeling states of each other" (p. 56). This description of the mother-daughter developmental relationship is consistent with descriptions given by Chodorow (1978), Friday (1977), and Gilligan and her colleagues (Gilligan, 1992; Gilligan et al., 1988, 1990). Implicitly and explicitly, these descriptions establish girls' and women's development and sense of self in contrast to boys' and men's development. Thus, an examination of earlier (male) descriptions of self and its development will be helpful in gaining clarity on the concept of a self-in-relation.

Conceptions of the Self

Most 20th century psychological theories of self and identity have at least some dependence on principles espoused by Sigmund Freud. Much of Freud's thinking about women was derived by applying wholesale, and without question, to women what he had observed in the lives and experiences of men; he also drew many unwarranted conclusions about children's experience from his observations of adult males. Within a few years after he began teaching his theories, some of his followers began to dispute his findings and the conclusions he derived from them. We will return to a discussion of Freud, his ideas about women, and the challenges of his disciples in Chapter 3. For now we will turn our attention to one of the most influential intellectual descendants of Freud, Erik Erikson. Erikson, like many of Freud's protégés, believed that social interaction had a much greater influence on personality formation than Freud's theories proposed.

Erikson and Ego Identity

Erikson (1950) was responsible for a major reformulation of Freud's theory of human development. This being the case, his ideas have also significantly influenced how contemporary psychologists think about female development. The critical feature of Erikson's work as it broke from its Freudian foundations was in its desire to demonstrate the social influence on and the interactional nature of developmental processes. He hoped to demonstrate that "social images and ... organismic forces" are not merely

> "'interrelated.' More than this: the mutual complementation of ethos and ego, of group identity and ego [individual] identity, puts a greater common potential at the disposal of both ego and social organization" (p. 23).

He stated that ego identity,

> "in its subjective sense, is the awareness of ... a selfsameness and continuity to the ego's synthesizing methods and that these methods are effective in safeguarding the sameness and continuity of one's meaning for others" (p. 22).

Given Erikson's (1950) insistence that identity is formed in a crucible of "social influence" and his definition of ego identity as including "selfsameness" and "continuity of one's meaning for others," it is curious that the concept of identity came to connote the oppositional self-assertion and separation—what I will call "over-against-ness"—that was deemed typical of the toddler or adolescent male vis-à-vis the parent, usually the mother. The common understanding that identity is expressed as over-against-ness may be based on a societal bias that places a high value on this type of functioning and assumes that "society" exists outside the home: the mother's sphere. However identity came to be equated with separateness and over-againstness, this was not a logical necessity. Erikson's understanding of identity is not at all incompatible with the more recent conception of the "self-in-relation" that has been proposed by Jordan et al. (1991).[2] Their use of "self-in-relation" is congruent with Erikson's concept of ego identity in its "selfsameness and continuity of method" (Erikson, 1950, p. 22). Further, it "effectively employs the method to safeguard one's meaning for others" (p. 22). What differs in development for a female, compared to development for a male, is that her environment is more centrally described by interpersonal relatedness and affect.

In the past females have been evaluated as having failed in achieving a mature sense of identity (Erikson, 1950, 1964, 1968).[3] Erikson described a model of psychosocial development of the self, containing eight stages that identified the milestones of each stage using success-failure dichotomies. Two milestones having special significance to thinking about women are "autonomy versus shame and self-doubt" which is resolved during early childhood and "identity versus identity diffusion" which is resolved during adolescence. He believed that female toddlers often exhibited signs of shame and self-doubt and that female adolescents were more likely than adolescent males to exhibit diffuse identity. It is intriguing that Erikson saw "shame and doubt" and other-embeddedness as evidence of failure to form identity, while Surrey (1991) saw "guilt and shame . . . [as evidence of] failure in mutual empathy" (p. 57) and as evidence that identity has formed successfully. This contradiction may be explained by the fact that shame has at least two meanings, modesty or shyness, and disgrace, though use of the former meaning is less common.[4]

Erikson (1968) suggested that in adolescence women "foreclose" on their futures because they have been less likely than men to define the self in terms of independence and professional goals; that they create a "moratorium" on separation because they have continued to define themselves in relation to significant others; and that, as a result of the previous two experiences, they have been less able to achieve lasting, healthy intimacy. Perhaps there is an alternative explanation: These females already have a healthy identity (which has a "selfsameness and continuity of method . . . [and] effectively employs the method to safeguard one's meaning for others") that forms in an environment different from that of males. They have already achieved healthy intimacy based in a different identity (Belenky et al., 1986; Chodorow, 1978; Friday, 1977; Gilligan, 1982; Gilligan et al., 1990; Jordan et al., 1991; Miller, 1976).

Using such an alternative explanation makes it clear that assessment of difference evaluated as negative, sick, immature, and even immoral is actually based on a priori assumptions about the value of independent and interdependent instrumental achievement in a public arena versus the value of interdependent and independent relational achievements in a private arena. The values, rather than the identity formation process, actually created the view that women were sick. Erikson (1950) himself, in a moment of social commentary, supplies a reason for this difference in valuation:

"[It is] a sad truth that in any system based on suppression, exclusion, and exploitation, the suppressed, excluded, and exploited unconsciously believe the evil image which they are made to represent by those who are dominant" (p. 30).

If we may accept Erikson's (1950) initial formulation of ego identity and Surrey's (1991) description of woman's self, then we can begin to describe a commensurate model of ego development that is true to many women's (as well as some men's) experience.[5] Surrey has identified and described men's identity as a "separate-self," while women's identity is a "related-self." If we start with this distinction, then we may ask what the predictable developmental crises are and how they might be resolved. Further, we might come to know how these concerns and achievements become voiced or silenced in the lives of girls and boys, men and women.

Hartmann and the Adaptive Ego

Hartmann (1958) is often regarded as the founder of "ego psychology." He emphasized the adaptive nature of ego functions, rather than their restrictive and conflict-resolving nature. He believed that there was a "conflict-free ego sphere" and that the mature ego may be more attached to reality than the infant ego is. His thought is important to the current discussion of women's identity formation because his concept of ego, like Erikson's, allows "adaptive" attachment to others as part of the individual's self definition, though historically theories have not used "ego" in this way.

Adaptation is the ego's achievement of successful interchange between the unconscious needs and demands of the personality and the environment. This is not necessarily conflict-free. Rather, it may be the result of the presence and successful resolution of conflict. But there may be conflict-free processes of adaptation. It is the task of the ego to mediate the demands of the unconscious (id and superego) and the external environment. The id constitutes those features of the personality that are biologic and/or instinctual, relate to drives and their satisfaction, and to the experience of pleasure. The superego expresses judging functions: observing, evaluating, and perfecting. It is as if the environment includes or excludes means for meeting the demands of the personality: the id says "all pleasure," the superego says "no pleasure," and the ego is left with the task of negotiating an adaptive resolution. By "adaptive" Hartmann seems to mean that which maintains the integrity of the personality, the realities of the environment, and a relationship between them. Ego strength, then, might be construed as an expression of the ego's capacity to maintain the person in its environment.

Adaptation is "reality mastery." According to Hartmann (1958), well-adapted means the person experiences

> "productivity, ... the ability to enjoy life, and ... [an undisturbed] mental equilibrium". [Adaptiveness must be measured] "with reference to environmental situations (on the average expectable—i.e., typical—situations, or on the average not expectable—i.e., atypical—situations)" and the organism's negotiation of them (p. 23).

There is a "state of adaptedness" and a "process of adaptedness" (p. 24).

> "[A]daptation ... is guaranteed ... on the one hand by primary equipment and the maturation of his apparatuses, and ... by those ego-regulated actions which ... counteract the disturbances in, and actively improve the person's relationship to, the environment" (p. 25).

Hartmann's description of ego function permits the formation of a self-in-relation as a perfectly normal and healthy manifestation of a woman's negotiation between her inner and outer realities. If it is the case that adaptation is the goal, then a self-in-relation is adaptive whenever and to the extent that it maintains the organism in relationship to the environment in a realistic way that allows for the satisfaction of internal and instinctual needs. In infancy, instinctual needs are always satisfied by a person who is other, to whom the infant must, at least in part, accommodate. Hartmann further suggested that adaptation is the mastery of reality and the search for and discovery of alternate realities. If males and females develop in different social environments that value maleness and femaleness differently, then it is not surprising that they exhibit adaptive differences in their ego functions. How men and women should develop is a separate issue. Acknowledging that difference exists does not address when or how the differences occur. For example, one intriguing question is: When does the primary caregiver become the instrumental, rather than the objectified, other?

Femininity and Shame

Jung and the Gendered Ego

Erikson and Hartmann both developed theories which were regarded as corrections or alternatives to the thinking of Freud. C. G. Jung also challenged Freud's conceptions and his claims to the universality of his observations. Jung disagreed with Freud in the construction and function of the unconscious, and in his understandings of human sexuality. Jung was not committed to biological determinism as was Freud, and he did not psychologize genital function in the same way that Freud did. Further, Jung had a more positive view of both the instincts and of the unconscious than did Freud (Singer, 1976).

For the purpose of gaining a more complete understanding of women's identity, several of Jung's constructs are relevant.[6] He understood the *ego* to be all conscious aspects of the individual's experience that form the basic sense of self, that is, "Me;" it is the central *complex* (a cluster of ideas and images with emotional valence) of consciousness. Jung defined the *shadow* as the aspects of the personality that the individual experiences as "not Me." The *unconscious* is *personal*, containing repressed ideas and images that are unique to the *individual,* and *collective*, containing repressed ideas and images (*Archetypes*) that are tribal, cultural, or universal to the human species. *Masculine* and *feminine* refer to beliefs, feelings and behaviors that are typically expressed by men and women, respectively, but may be expressed by persons of either sex. The *Masculine* and *Feminine Archetypes* exist in the mental lives of both women and men.

Jung conceived of ego-functioning in a way that would currently be viewed as male-biased because he valued the masculine over the feminine and defined ego and individuation (the maturing process) in terms of masculine consciousness. However, Jung proposed a model of personality in which maturity was described as the integration into consciousness of feminine attributes by men and of masculine attributes by women. He expanded the description of healthy personality functioning to include aspects of contrasexual traits in each of the sexes, thus alleviating some of the biological determinism of Freud. He also highlighted the presence and the potentially positive nature of the *anima* (the unconscious feminine in males) and the *animus* (the unconscious masculine in females) that reside in the personal unconscious. C. G. Jung (1933/1971) described the feminine and the anima in terms of relatedness and receptivity, and the masculine and the animus in terms of separateness and penetration. The *Anima* and

Animus are expressions of the archetype of the Soul (Ellenberger, 1970; E. Jung, 1972; Singer, 1972, 1976). E. Jung's work is significant for this inquiry because it is an early positive description of the differences and similarities of men's and women's identities and identity formation that is based in some awareness that the meanings of sex and gender are socially constructed. They were among the first 20th century theorists to place positive value on individuals assimilating personality features of the opposite sex into one's conscious functioning. While Jung incorporated nonbiological understandings of sex-role functioning in his concept of identity, his basic conception had much in common with those of Freud, Erikson, Hartmann and many other theorizers of the early and middle 20th century. Until recently, the concepts of ego, self, and identity in western culture, and in western psychology, have been consistently described as separate, independent, individualistic, bounded, masterful and empty (Bellah, Madsen, Sullivan, Swindler, & Tipton, 1985; Cushman, 1990; Gilligan, 1982; Jordan et al., 1991; Lasch, 1978; Sampson, 1978, 1993).

Critiques of the Concept of the Bounded, Masterful Self

A growing number of authors have challenged traditional conceptions of the self as separate, bounded, and masterful (Bellah et al., 1985; Cushman, 1990; Kobayashi, 1989; Lasch, 1978). Cushman believes that the socially-constructed "bounded, masterful self" (p. 599) has emerged in western thought as "a self that has specific psychological boundaries, an internal locus of control, and a wish to manipulate the external world for its own personal ends" (p. 600). Further, he describes this self as an "empty self" and claims that this particular construction of the self was created in response to a particular set of economic and political needs that arose as consequences of industrialization and the world wars such that people needed to need the nonessentials that society produced. According to Sampson (1993), it is this bounded, masterful, manipulative, self-serving, empty self that is being deconstructed by some contemporary psychologists, and by individuals and groups who are involved in certain political movements that have in common what Sampson calls

"*identity politics*, a politics based on the particular life experiences of people who seek to be in control of their own identities and subjectivities and who claim that socially dominant groups have denied them this opportunity" (p. 1219).

It is common for these groups to claim that they "have been denied voice in establishing the conditions of [their lives]" (p. 1219). Many members of these movements characterize responses to their challenges as accommodative; they believe that adding on the underrepresented groups does not transform the cultural environment in which life is lived because the additions are "not seen as constitutive of the phenomenon of interest" (p. 1220). The feminist critique that Sampson cites is particularly relevant to the current discussion: Under current conditions "[i]f women are to be heard, they must speak like men, constructing themselves in the very manner in which they have been constructed by dominant male interests, desires, and fears" (p. 1220).

Sampson (1993) states that the most basic categories western culture and the discipline of psychology use to identify people, such as the terms "men" and "women," are being challenged. The categories themselves "perform social actions" (Edwards, 1991, p. 523) that determine how the members of the category are viewed. According to Sampson (1993), most of our current categories of identity are dualistic.

> "[T]hese 'social' divisions of persons' identity are not seen to be natural categories covered by the story of either biology or genetics, even though the latter have increasingly become the discursive means by which such divisions gain their current legitimacy" (pp. 1222–3).

Thus, the setting of categories of discourse and defining them is an exercise of power. Sampson states that "without their own voice ... [the voiceless groups] will continue to be complicit in their own domination" (p. 1223). The presentation of the problems of voice and voicelessness in the underclasses is compelling. However, as each group speaks in its own voice, each becomes complicit in the domination of every other group and in the rejection of discourse with every other but the members of its own class.[7] Sampson, along with Gilligan (1990), raises several points for consideration by those who practice the discipline of psychology, I will highlight only one: Dialogue. Sampson states that one cannot truly have a voice if the other will not hear, and that dialogue requires "a meeting among variously positioned standpoints, among persons who have equal say in the discursive processes out of which their joint realities are constructed." The question remains at this time: How will the "meeting ... [of] their joint realities" occur? Recent findings of object relations theorists and adolescent developmentalists provide some clues.

Together and Apart: Building a Case for Wholeness

Commonly held views of identity development in American psychology assume the primacy of separateness and autonomy as markers of healthy, mature adult functioning (Cushman, 1990; Gilligan; 1982; Miller, 1976); but, recently there have been many challenges to this definition. While some challenges arise from philosophical critiques of the intellectual discipline of psychology and others arise from political critiques of the ideological commitments that ground the practice of psychology, still others arise from more pragmatic endeavors investigating how infants and adolescents develop.

Adolescence: Time to Separate in Connection

According to many who study adolescent behavior and development, understandings of the adolescent and the role of the family during adolescence are changing (Archer, 1993; Bell & Bell, 1983; Cooper, Grotevant, & Condon, 1983; Grotevant & Cooper, 1986; Kroger & Archer, 1993; Reis, Olevinci, & Curd, 1983; White, Speisman, & Costos, 1983; Youniss, 1983). In the past, many researchers have described the developmental life task of the adolescent as one of increasing separation from the family of origin, often in ways that are viewed as aggressively distancing (Erikson, 1968). Other theorists and researchers objected to the portrayal of adolescence as a period of turbulence; they presented data suggesting that adolescence is a period in which the adolescent's relations with the family, and especially the parents, continue much as they did earlier in childhood, claiming that growing distance between the adolescent and the family, especially hostile distance, was an unusual occurrence and indicated pathology. As an example of this emerging focus I will outline one investigation reported by Grotevant and Cooper (1986). They suggest that data from the fields of family sociology, family therapy, psychiatry, and developmental psychology are converging to reveal a description of the adolescent as one who makes increasing efforts to understand and express her or his uniqueness as an individual while remaining connected to an interpersonal environment that continues to support, contain, model, and reinforce independent and intimate behaviors. They state that "the parent-adolescent relationship is transformed considerably as it is renegotiated by the parent and the adolescent" (p. 82). Citing the work of Kandel and Lesser (1969), they conclude that increasing expression of autonomy during adolescence is not disengagement. In fact, those adolescents who expressed the greatest feelings of autonomy were more likely to describe their parents as close, valued guides who were perceived as role models.

After presenting a careful review of the literature, Grotevant and Cooper (1986) suggest that the developmental life task of adolescence is to elaborate and refine the continuing interplay between individuality and interpersonal connection within the environmental contexts of family and peers. They suggested that adolescents in helpful environments will be able to explore potential identities and will become increasingly able to commit to a coherent sense of self; they defined exploration as the presence of role-taking behaviors and commitment as the presence of expressed unique viewpoints.

Grotevant and Cooper (1986) identified four distinct interpersonal factors which determine the success of negotiations of the life task in "normal" families: (a) Empathy, the capacity to be mutually sensitive to individual family members, to respect each person, and to act in general support of others; (b) permeability, the capacity to respond to the ideas of another, giving both permission and encouragement for the others' establishing a particular point-of-view; (c) recognition of difference (separateness), demonstrated by requests for action, direct disagreement, irrelevant comments, and indirect disagreement; and (d) direct suggestion of action for the other. They proposed that individuated families would demonstrate "moderate to high levels of expressed individuality (especially separateness) in the context of at least moderate levels of connectedness (through empathy and permeability)" (p. 91). They found that families who function according to the above definition had adolescents who demonstrated high levels of identity expression and high levels of role-taking skill. They concluded that adolescent identity formation must be understood in terms of development of autonomy and connection.[8]

The work of other developmentists also highlight the role of connection in adolescent identity formation (Apter, 1990; Baumrind, 1982, 1987; Gilligan et al., 1988; Josselson, 1987; Kroger, 1993; Kroger & Archer, 1993; Lapsley, 1990). In particular, Josselson (1986, 1987, 1992) has summarized the various strands of research on separateness and connectedness in order to formulate a life developmental model of attachment that in some ways parallels the stage theory of Erikson.[9] Unlike Erikson's model, Josselson's (1992) model explicitly describes movement between the ways of attachment as fluid, and she carefully emphasizes that all ways of being attached continue to find expression in the experience of individuals throughout the entire life span. "As each dimension emerges in the developmental history of the individual, each is concrete and basic. As development proceeds, each way of connecting becomes more symbolic, less physical and spatial, but no less crucial" (Josselson, 1992, p. 6).

Josselson (1992) describes eight modes of attachment, or ways "in which we overcome the space between us" (p. 6). *Holding* is an important part of the life of the infant, and the need to be held continues to express itself throughout the life course; the first *attachment* takes place early in life between infant and mother, and multiple attachments form over a lifetime. *Passionate experience* is the expression of the infant's initial quest for pleasure and gratification and finds later expression in sexual union and other bliss-filled experiences. *Eye-to-eye validation* [10] is another early experience of connection in the life of the infant that is communicated by the mirroring-mother. Later in early childhood *idealization and identification* become important sources of connection to the powerful others who inhabit the child's universe, and they allow the child both to have present and to become the important other. *Mutuality* becomes possible as the child becomes more aware of the uniqueness of the other and of the possibilities of engaging them in shared experiences. The growing child gains a sense of the self as being embedded in the interpersonal arenas in which she or he lives, and, at adolescence, the concern to develop a sense of belonging and awareness of fit with those communities gives rise to practicing differentiation and communality. Finally, the capacity to *tend and care* for others, which has been present in nascent forms all along, becomes a way in which the young adult seeks to connect with the larger world, making a commitment to what and who to look after. As the individual continues through life's course, he or she finds these modes of connection continue to structure and enhance experience. According to Josselson, these expressions of relatedness coexist and act as point and counterpoint to expressions of separateness. To understand human experience, one must recognize the presence and activity of separateness and relatedness *and* their interaction.

Beginning with Connection

Blatt and Blass (1990) have critiqued Erikson's stage theory, suggesting the "importance of formulating a dialectical developmental model that describes the interaction between attachment and separation and between product and process" (p. 107). They state that one can view all models of psychological development as arising from one of two starting points, estrangement or union. In the former, the infant is perceived as arriving in the world estranged and in need of forming attachment; in the latter, it is perceived as arriving united with the mother and in need of developing separateness. Most well-known theorists of human development take as their premise that the infant begins life in union with the mother and proceed to espouse models that describe development in terms of increased separateness, autonomy, independence, etc. However, it is possible to argue for a model that assumes "attachment and attempt[s] to understand the development of the individual as a unit in interaction" (Blatt & Blass, 1990, p. 109). In such models (proposed by Ainsworth, 1982, 1989; Balint, 1934/1952, 1937/1952; Fairbairn, 1952; Guntrip, 1989; Winnicott, 1971) "the gestalt [is] past and present interpersonal relationships. . . . [and] the emergence of intimacy, dependence, care, and affection is the subject of study" (Blatt & Blass, 1990, p. 109).

In order to describe the dialectical model, Guisinger and Blatt (1994) first review the concept of individuality. Development of the concept of individualism as a primary social form is associated with "the emergence of participatory societies" (p. 105). There are four distinct individualistic psychologies which have currency in western thought— romantic, egoistic, ideological, and alienated individualisms.[11] These four systems share "a fundamental egocentric bias. The individual is not viewed as an integral part of his or her social world; the feeling of belonging to a group is not seen as giving life purpose and direction" (p. 105). Guisinger and Blatt (1994) suggest that, in contrast to the individualistic psychologies, a growing body of evidence argues strongly for a relational bias in human development. For example: Evolutionary biology describes prosocial, cooperative and helping behaviors among animals; infant research documents the presence of prosocial behavior, strong emotional attachments, and intense ongoing desire to form interpersonal bonds in infants and children; and cross-cultural psychology depicts the function of tribal communities as "ensembled individualism."

Guisinger and Blatt (1994) suggest that
individuality and relatedness appear to develop in a relatively independent process until mid- or late adolescence (although a case could be made for an earlier interrelationship). At this point, these

lines become dialectically interrelated and integrated in the formation of what Erikson (1950) has called *identity*. (p. 108)

This formulation raises two issues for the authors: (a) The need for society to foster the formation of stable, interacting living groups, giving special attention to the formation of community, in order to encourage, social as well as personal self-interest; and (b) the need for society to foster the development of relatedness in men and to validate the skills of relatedness that women have, which has implications for the roles of fathers in the family and the community. In summary, Guisinger and Blatt (1994) argue for voicing relatedness and the value of relatedness in order to achieve models of development and interpersonal practices that bring about more personal wholeness in the members of the human family.

Voice, Language, and Identity Formation

Three recent discussions of voice (Lovinger, 1994; Schneider, 1994; Tabin, 1994) and one earlier discussion of language development (Cameron & Magaret, 1951) help elucidate the meaning and power of voice, both explicitly and metaphorically.

Language and Speech

Cameron and Magaret (1951) refer to the uniquely social character of voice when they state that language is an outcome rather than a source of communication, and that "[c]ommunication arises out of need" (p. 88). Language is formed in an environment of "cooperation and reciprocity" (p. 89). In order for language to develop the infant must be biosocially ready and there must be an older, language-competent other available to provide language resources to the infant. Advances in the use of language occur because of complex feedback and reinforcing processes that include the infant's own vocal behaviors and the vocal behaviors of the other. In addition, language development occurs in an affect-laden environment in which the older person initially expresses great pleasure at the infant's vocal behaviors. Thus, language production is experienced as an emotionally charged and socially shared event that is very satisfying to the infant.

As the infant practices and gains environmental experiences, she or he learns that certain sounds belong to certain objects, actions, and relationships. The infant first learns to indicate the association of words to relationships, objects and actions, and later learns to symbolize those objects, relationships, and actions by the words. With the achievement of symbolization, the infant can begin to explore and elaborate the world of the unreal as well as the world of the real. The infant will develop a "self-attitude and [a] self-response" (Cameron & Magaret, 1951, p. 97) which in turn will allow the infant to learn self-evaluation. At the same time, the infant is discovering silent speech; and with it comes

> [t]he transformation of public, communicative speech into private, unshared thinking . . . one of the most powerful agencies in bringing about the socialization of human individuals. . . . [L]inguistic forms of thinking [allow] the ghosts of a person's secret past to rail against him or urge [her] on to unmerited applause. (pp. 105–106)

One example of this development that is particularly appropriate to this study is given:

> The child's sex is highly significant [to him or her for] later identification and therefore operates selectively on the development of self-evaluation. The mother stresses her own ideal of femininity in guiding her little girl's daily conduct, and of masculinity in bringing up her little boy. Contrasts and comparisons are repeatedly voiced which reinforce one behavior and negatively affect the other. . . . He learns to value highly the things he must do as a little man, and to disparage the domestic and maternal achievements of his sister. . . . And he learns to give [these messages] to himself. (p. 104)

The child creates[12] a sexed self, described in his or her own words, but made up from the words of valued others in the child's environment. Even later, the child discovers that she can say one thing and do another; that she can think one thing while speaking another; and that she can speak to her silently so that only he can hear. With these achievements the child becomes more and more able to be what he or she is not in response to the pressures and demands of important others in the social environment. "The human being learns to deceive himself as well as the other, to divide his own behavior into contradicting systems, and in extreme instances, to disown his reactions and ascribe them to real or fictitious [others]" (Cameron & Magaret, 1951, p. 109). Thus, the child moves on from the creation of a personal identity to the creation of false identities as well. Accordingly, the child is able to create not just a self, but many selves.

The Wordless Voice

Tabin (1994) has been interested in nonverbal uses of voice. She states that voice is laden with affect that is expressed by tone, pitch, volume, and rate. Because the affect may be unconscious, the voice gives clues to inner states of experience. She also reflects on the power of silence—of voicelessness—to communicate who a person is and what they experience of the world.

Lovinger (1994), by focusing on the use of voice in fostering mother-infant attachment, also comments on the nonverbal, but communicative, facets of speech. The mother, then later the child, use the voice, apart from the words spoken, to initiate and regulate attachment, to engage attention, and to impart affect and motive. The child communicates profoundly with sound, regarding her sense of self and her sense of the other.

In his response to the previous presentations, Schneider (1994) emphasizes the importance of the ear. He reflects on voice and ear from the perspective of the clinician, stating that for the patient, as for the child, the primary task is to "hear the other into speech" (Morton, 1985). The other person needs to be listened to so that they may listen to themselves. Further, Schneider suggested that a patient's "outpouring of material," which leaves the therapist feeling confused and concerned, is the patient's "own state of confusion and concern" (p. 9), the patient's inner experience of his concern over his own identity.

Cameron and Magaret (1951), Tabin (1994), Lovinger (1994), and Schneider (1994) each explain the ways in which voice creates, as well as expresses, identity: Conscious identity, unconscious affect identity, attachment identity, feared identity, heard identity, and silenced identity. Further, they each have suggested that, in addition to verbal language, the child is given and creates an affect language which is extremely powerful in creating the child's meanings of self.[13] No wonder, then, that "voice" has become such a powerful metaphor for the capacity to express who and what we are.

Conclusion

According to many researchers, men and women develop and experience different senses of self. For a variety of reasons that apply in western culture, it appears that men, as a group, develop a sense of self that depends on an awareness of separateness from others, while women, as a group, develop a sense of self that depends on awareness of connection to others. These selves tend to find different expressions in culture, and are used by the culture differently. For example, women provide the majority of care for young children, the elderly, the sick, and the dying (Bregman & Thiermann, 1995; Faludi, 1991; Miller, 1987); even when both partners of a marriage work outside the home for pay, women do most of the housework; and men provide the majority of leadership in the workplace, whether the workplace is a business, a school, or a church (Faludi, 1991; Miller, 1987). According to Wallis (1989), women have been evaluating their gains and losses at the end of two waves of feminism. They are dissatisfied with the results and believe that they have been cheated. They believe that they do "men's work" now, but have all the "women's work" to do as well.

In the 1970s and 1980s, theorists and practitioners in business, psychology and education believed that increased autonomy and assertiveness in women's self-perception and social behavior would increase their social status and their physical and social well-being (Faludi, 1991; Friedan, 1963; Hennig & Jardim, 1976). However, several indicators suggest that increases in autonomy and self-determination in women have not brought about significant changes in attitudes toward women and women's roles (Faludi, 1991). The incidence of rape, domestic violence, divorce, and poverty in the lives of American women is rising, suggesting a continuing negative valorization of women in society (Faludi, 1991). These factors negatively impact women's sense of well-being and social status regardless of their self-definitions. Perhaps it is not enough to increase women's autonomy and independence. Changes in the value placed on "women's work" and on femininity must also occur. It appears that for women to have a voice, they must speak their experience, and those around them must hear it.

Currently, many scholars are critiquing the concept of the separate, autonomous self, and the models of development that describe its formation. Some are even questioning the existence of a separate, autonomous self. Data from research in evolutionary biology and infant research demonstrate that animals and children have and express innate capacities for prosocial and relational behavior. Cross-cultural psychologists describe a model of community relationship called ensembled individualism. Developmentalists are finding it necessary to revise theory as evidence mounts that adolescents form their sense of autonomy within family relationships that are characterized by mutuality, empathy, permeability, and trust. In the field of object relations, scholars are reconstructing psychoanalytic theories to account for the spontaneously expressed desire for relatedness that appears throughout the life of the infant and the young child. Finally, researchers and clinicians who are interested in language, speech, and voice production give vital clues to how voice expresses identity within relationship. It appears likely that relatedness and separateness have a much more complicated and interwoven relationship to each other in their roles in the development of identity than the one described by Erikson's (1950) stage theory (Blatt & Blass, 1990; Blass & Blatt, 1992; Guisinger & Blatt, 1994; Josselson, 1992).

While theorists and investigators in the academic community describe the benefits of relatedness and interpersonal connection for men as well as women, other reports appear in the popular press. Men's solitude and aggressiveness are "hardwired" (Moir & Jessel, 1991); "men are from Mars, and women are from Venus" (Gray, 1992); and women are eager to be led by their husbands (Promisekeepers, 1994); woman is a profoundly sexual being in her embodiedness (Paglia, 1990).[14] Each proponent of these arguments implies or states that there is an essential nature in women that is different from an essential nature in men, and these popular arguments are selling extremely well. The image of man as autonomous and independent, separate and assertive is a common and popular myth, as is the image of woman as related and gentle.

For several centuries it has been the case that manly separateness has been valued more highly than womanly relatedness. More recently masculine aggressiveness and men have been vilified (D'Antonio, 1994; Miedzian, 1991). Behavioral definitions of gender that attribute masculinity to men and femininity to women—including, ironically, the definition of woman's identity as self-in-relation (Belenky et al., 1986; Gilligan, 1982; Jordan et al., 1991) continue to hold powerful sway. In the past, insistence that women are feminine and men are masculine created difficulties that have led to an ongoing problem of females' "voicelessness."

Voice has been defined, in this work, as self-declaration in an interpersonal context that has a primary goal of maintaining interpersonal connection. This voice is not necessarily oppositional nor aggressive. In order to gain a better understanding of what women (and men?) are and are not declaring, it will be necessary to undertake a study of masculinity and femininity, sex and gender. With these terms defined it will become possible to determine what in women's experience is voiced or silenced, and in what contexts. Sex and gender, masculinity and femininity are the focus of the next chapter.

Chapter 2.
Gender: Feminine and Masculine Defined

"I walked into the room and his eyes opened wide, his eyebrows raised. He loved the way I looked; so so did I. I felt *sooo* feminine."
A woman's comment about her therapist during a session

"He kept talking about my being the "target for some man-arrow to bull's-eye." I didn't get it! Then, he tried a different analogy: something about Jung and alchemy; how the pregnant belly is like the alchemist's oven, that making babies is a symbol for transformation of the psyche. I finally decided that I didn't understand because he was giving the *man's view* of the "feminine." I realized, since I'm a woman, I'd have to come up with my own."
A woman's comment about her therapist's interpretation

In recent years it has been suggested that gender is a constructed reality,[1] implying that there is no intrinsic requirement that human experience be sexualized in any way (Butler, 1990; Elliot, 1991).[2] Despite this challenge, there has been relative agreement in western culture for many years about definitions of "masculine" and "feminine." These two adjectives often have been considered as representing opposite and mutually exclusive features of human personality and behavior which exist on a single continuum, so that to be more masculine is to be less feminine and vice-versa.[3] Further, it has been assumed that masculinity resides in male persons, while femininity resides in female persons. Recent attempts to relocate masculine and feminine functions in all human persons (that is, reconstructing the terms of gendered human nature as psychosocial "androgyny")[4] have had limited success.

Any investigation must begin with definitions, but in the case of "masculinity" and "femininity," definitions are even more crucial than might be so generally. The complexity of thought, the confounding of the physical and nonphysical aspects of personhood, and the complicated history of social relations between women and men which surround these two terms have created intolerable obfuscation.

Merriam-Webster's Collegiate Dictionary (1993), defines *feminine* as

    1: **female**; 2: characteristic of or appropriate or unique to women; 3: of, relating to, or constituting the gender that ordinarily includes most words or grammatical forms referring to females. . . .

and

    1a: a noun, pronoun, adjective, or inflectional form or class of the feminine gender; b: the feminine gender; 2: the feminine principle" (p. 428);

and *masculine* as

    1a: **MALE**; b: having qualities appropriate to or usu. associated with a man; 2: of, relating to, or constituting the gender that ordinarily includes most words of grammatical forms referring to males. . . .
    1: the masculine gender; 2: a noun, pronoun, adjective, or grammatical form or class of the masculine gender; 3: a male person (p. 714).

According to the *Oxford Dictionary of English Etymology* (Onions, Friedrichson, & Burchfield, 1976), the word *feminine* derives from the Latin root *felare,* to suck or to suckle, while the word *masculine* derives from the Old French *masle* from the Latin, *masculinus,* meaning *male.* The word *male* means "pertaining to the sex that begets offspring," while the word *female* means "of the sex which produces offspring." As can be seen from the definitions, the terms "feminine" and "masculine" have been closely linked to biological sex linguistically. Sex (male, female) is part of the definition of masculine and feminine; however, the terms have been used primarily as signifiers for nonbiological, personological traits of human nature at least throughout the 20th century.

Gender and Sex

In gender- and sex-role research it has become increasingly common to treat masculinity and femininity as two separate continua of human experience (Bem, 1974, 1975; Doyle & Paludi, 1985).[5] According to this formulation, any individual may express high or low masculinity and high or low femininity without necessary correspondence between expressed gender and biological sex. Thus, gender-identity or gender-role function will be expressed according to the possibilities in Table 1.

Table 1. Gender Identification and Expression

Gender	Masculine	
	Low	High
Feminine		
Low	undifferentiated	masculine
High	feminine	androgyny* (masculine *and* feminine)

*Bem (1974) called this combination "androgyny" [see note 4 above]

This model casts doubt on common understandings that males should express only masculinity while females should express only femininity, and raises questions about the relationship between sex and gender.

Sex

Following the report of Doyle and Paludi (1985), the word *sex* is defined as that characteristic of the organism which is determined by the presence of primary and secondary physiological traits and by relative levels of reproductive hormones in the human body. Human beings are generally identified as being one of two sexes, male or female, assigned on the basis of genetic, physiological and/or hormonal traits. However, even biological sex (maleness and femaleness) is found to be present in varying and interacting ways in any given individual (see Table 2).

Table 2. Contributing Factors to Current Popular Understandings of Feminine and Masculine

Category variables	Maleness or masculinity	Femaleness or femininity
Biology[a]		
Genitalia	penis, testes, scrotum seminal vesicles vas deferens	clitoris, vagina, labia vulva, uterus, ovaries
Voice	deep	high
Hair (body/facial)	more	less
Muscle mass	more	less
Fat	brown/less	white/more
Hormones		
Estrogen	2°	1°
Androgen	1°	2°
Parenting Roles	"fathering"	"mothering"
(confounded within the category)	—guidance —defense —provision	—nurturance —warmth —care
Social Sphere		
public	BOSS[b]	worker
private	husband	WIFE, MOTHER[b]
Personality		
behavior	instrumentality	expressiveness
attributes	tough, aggressive, powerful	soft, tender, vulnerable
attitudes	objectivity	subjectivity

[a]The presence of these characteristics is highly variable. Men differ from one another in the extent of presence of these traits; as do women. Comparative differences between men and women is relative.

[b]Upper case represents the primary and desired goal identity according to traditional social formulas; lower case represents alternate identities that may occur, but not as highly valued.

For example: Individual human beings who have genital characteristics of both sexes (hermaphrodites), or who have indeterminate genital features, are present in the population in very small numbers. Other rare individuals have genetic sex determinants which are different from their genital structures (Doyle & Paludi, 1985). Most human adults are relatively easily assigned to a sex category on the basis of cursory observation. Often, the discriminating features are naturally occurring biological sex traits, such as beard or breasts.

In some cases, discriminating features are changed or enhanced by artificial manipulation of physiological features in order to achieve conformity to some highly socially valued standard (Doyle & Paludi, 1985; Fine-Thomas, 1993; Wolf, 1992).

The word *sex* is derived from an Old English root, *seks*, to cut or sever or separate (Barnhart, 1988; Onions et al., 1976). This derivation suggests that in the development of the English language, there was, at some time, a growing awareness of difference between men and women that brought about a separation in thinking about them. Another possibility is that the word is rooted in an experience of sexual intercourse as an analog of cutting or being cut. The word is a fairly recent addition to the language, first used in the Wycliffe Bible in the 15th century, and coming into common usage in the 19th century.

Gender

Gender is a word even more recently assigned as a category describing human nature. It derives from the Latin verb, *generare* which means "to generate, to produce, to engender"; or from the Latin noun, *genus* or *generis* which means "descent or origin" (Onions et al., 1976). According to *Webster's New World Dictionary* (1964) *gender*
> has been (and is) used in linguistics and grammar as the classification by which nouns and pronouns (and often accompanying modifiers) are grouped and inflected, or changed in form, in relation to sex or their lack of it; gender is *natural* when, as in English, Persian and Armenian, animate beings and inanimate things are classified as masc., fem., and neuter (e.g., man, masc; woman, fem; tree, neuter); gender is *grammatical* when, as in the majority of languages possessing it, beings and things are classified according to remotely animistic, psychological or formal associations (e.g., Anglo-Saxon *wif* or German *weib*, woman, neuter; Latin *fluvius*, river, masc. [but Latin *flumen*, stream, neut.]; Latin *pirus*, pear tree, fem.): English, now virtually free from noun inflection, shows gender chiefly by pronoun reference. (p. 602)

Two additional relevant definitions include:
> *gender* "2a: SEX . . . b: the behavioral, cultural, or psychological traits typically associated with one sex;"

and
> *gendered*: reflecting the experience, prejudices, or orientations of one sex more than the other"

(*Merriam-Webster's Collegiate Dictionary*, 1993, p. 484).

Beginning in the 1970s, gender has been used in psychological and sociological research of sex roles to mean "the social, cultural, and psychological aspects that pertain to traits, norms, stereotypes, and roles considered typical and desirable for those whom society has designated as female or male" (Doyle & Paludi, 1985, p. 5), and referred to the words "masculine" and "feminine" (Bem, 1974). The *Publication Manual of the American Psychological Association* (1994), states, "*Gender* is cultural and is the term to use when referring to men and women as social groups. *Sex* is biological; use it when the biological distinction is predominant" (p. 47). That is, the word gender connotes nonbiological features of human nature that have been assigned to groups designated by terms defined by biological categories.[6] However, this use of "gender," "man," and "woman" creates difficulty since *Merriam-Webster's Collegiate Dictionary* (1993) defines "man" as "an adult male human" (p. 705); and "woman" as "an adult female person" (p. 1360). Using words that are defined by biological attributes to designate "social groups" leaves the meanings of the words, and all discussions using them, hopelessly confounded. To use terms (man, woman) that are commonly understood to represent biological difference in order to indicate group membership that is socially determined and nonbiological traits that both sexes may exhibit (such as behavior, feeling, and belief) is to further confuse an area which needs clarification. Defining "gender" in a way that disentangles purely physical sex characteristics from other human attributes is extremely important; however, using "gender" to refer to "men and women as social groups" does not accomplish this goal.[7]

Colloquially, "gender" is increasingly used as a synonym for "sex," but this colloquialism leads to serious misunderstandings in all discussions of men and women and their various roles and tasks. For example, a recent personnel application read:

> Gender: male _____ female _____

Is the application asking about gender or sex?

Let me offer another example: the title of a recently published book, *Gender War, Gender Peace: The Quest for Love and Justice Between Men and Women* (Kipnis & Herron, 1994), uses "gender" to restate the cliché "war between the sexes" (p. 11). Is the battle between man and woman (i.e., sexed beings), or between men and women (i.e., social groups) or between masculinity and femininity (i.e., gender) or between men and women over gender or between people over gender or between people over sex? Here is another example from the popular press from the extremely popular book, *Men Are from Mars; Women Are from Venus*, in which Gray (1992) consistently associates nonsexual behavior with the sex of the actors: he describes men (Martians) as problem-solvers and women (Venutians) as advice-givers, suggesting total species alienation one from the other without giving explanations for the supposed differences.

Other evidence of the need for clarification is found in current research on differences between men and women (for example, Belenky et al., 1986; Farrell, 1988; Gilligan, 1982; Gilligan et al., 1988, 1990; Jordan et al., 1991) that states conclusions which attribute gender qualities to representatives or groups identified by sex (e.g., the "ethic of care" is women's way of making moral decisions because many women and fewer men use these processes). What is often unclear in current literature and research is to what extent the "woman's" or "man's" way is due to femaleness or maleness per se, rather than being due to some other complex of variables that exist across and within the boundaries of group membership. The further problem of inadvertently overstating between group differences also becomes more likely.

A common mistake which has led to misrepresentations of women and men in many theories of human psychology in the past has been to equate sex and gender. Using "man," "men," "woman," or "women" or the "generic, Man" has serious repercussions when that use implies that certain behaviors, feelings and beliefs occur because the actor is a given sex, even though the sex of the actor does not directly determine or limit expression of the traits. While it is probably not possible to fully separate the social, cultural, and psychological realms of experience that are typically conflated in discussions of sex and gender, some attempt must be made to discriminate between them (see Figure 1).).

36 Femininity and Shame

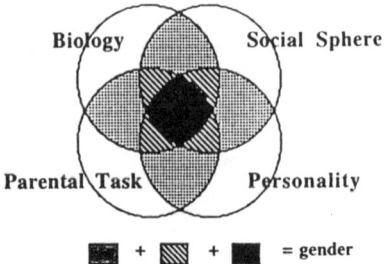

a. Traditional definitions = confounded gender

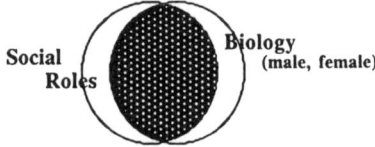

b. Current Definition = confounded gender

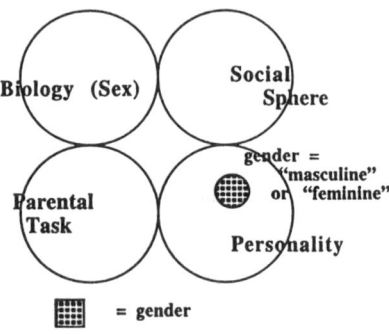

c. Unconfounded gender

Figure 1. Variables which are confounded in operational definitions of gender: (a) traditional definition; (b) current definition of gender as "men" or "women" as social groups; (c) unconfounded definition of gender as a personality variable.

Gender: Feminine and Masculine Defined

Understanding gender (the masculine and the feminine) involves distinguishing four correlated areas of human experience. One source of confound in understanding gender is biology; it has been common to construct psychological understandings of gender based upon reflection on the functions of concrete body parts associated with biological maleness and femaleness; Freud's concept of penis envy is a common example of this practice. This confusion is associated with the incorrect assumption that genital body parts determine cognitive, affective, and behavioral choices. Due to this over-concretization of genital sexuality as definitive of gender-identity, it has been believed that men must be attentive to the external world and intrude upon it just as an erect penis extends into and intrudes on an external person-object, and that women must attend to the inner world and receive into it just as a vaginal canal and a bag-shaped uterus wait to be intruded upon in a hidden place within the woman's body.

A second source of confound of the labels—gender, masculine and feminine—lies in the cultural understanding when there is an over-reliance on social and biological aspects of parenting to give meaning to them. That is, a confound occurs when gender is understood through an understanding of fathering and mothering, and, especially through the mother's role as physical carrier of the fetus within the uterus and physical nourisher of the infant first by the umbilical cord and then by the breast. On the contrary, parental role is designated largely by the performance of nonsexually determined care giving tasks, rather than by biological fatherhood or motherhood. "Mother" and "father" become merely labels or names. The view of gender through biological maternal function also over-concretizes personality in the body and in biological functions, even though most parenting tasks do not depend on the sex of the care provider.

A third source of confound in working definitions of masculine and feminine is conflation of gender with location in social sphere. In the 19th and 20th centuries, it has been common to associate women and the feminine with the private sphere of home and family, and men and the masculine with the public sphere of job and marketplace. For example, Levinson (1994) reports that, culturally, woman's identity has been related to whether or not she marries; accordingly, her sense of self is closely associated to the "traditional marriage enterprise" (p. 14) and the work that occurs in that context. Also, consider the comments made in a review of the Disney (1937/1993) movie version of *Snow White*: "Snow White never lifts a finger to direct her fate. . . . All she does in return is cook and clean for seven" (Brooks, 1993). In these examples there is an implicit assumption that what happens in the private sphere has no impact on the public sphere, that it is not valuable, and that it does not require initiative, drive, or independence. Certainly, one objects to a fate of doing only housework, but to suggest that "Snow White never lifts a finger" is to distort the reality of the private sphere; having a comfortable and healthy home takes effort and requires many of the same management skills required in the marketplace. Definitions of gender relying on social spheres confound biological and personality traits with the typical contexts in which the traits are expressed. That is, biology and personality are confused with where one spends her time.

Table 3. Masculine and Feminine Descriptors From the Bem Sex-Role Inventory

Masculine	**Feminine**
Leadership abilities	Soft spoken
Aggressive	Affectionate
Athletic	Cheerful
Ambitious	Childlike
Analytical	Compassionate
Assertive	Feminine
Competitive	Shy
Forceful	Flatterable
Defends own beliefs	Gentle
Dominant	Gullible
Makes decisions easily	Warm
Independent	Yielding
Self-reliant	Tender
Self-sufficient	Loyal,
Strong personality	Sympathetic
Masculine	Understanding
Willing to take a stand	Does not use harsh language
Willing to take risks	Eager to soothe hurt feelings
Individualistic	Loves Children
Acts like a leader	Sensitive to the needs of others

Note. Descriptors from "The measurement of psychological androgyny," by S. L. Bem, 1974, *Journal of Consulting and Clinical Psychology, 42,* 156.

A fourth source of confound occurs when gender is described as feelings, attitudes and behaviors that have been considered representative of human personality but then is assigned to individuals according to biological sex. For example, some personality characteristics identified by Bem (1974) have been differentially associated with members of each sex (see Table 3): Men, but not women, are viewed as strong or assertive, athletic, and independent; women, but not men, are viewed as weak or gentle, affectionate, and gullible.

While there may be biological influences on the expression of a few traits (like aggression), the traits are not essentially sexed, and the biological effects on the traits are not sole, or even primary, determinants of them.[8] Gender identity, as it is experienced by any individual human person, is shaped by a complex and subtle interaction of many contributing variables which belong to these four overlapping realms of human experience, biology, social sphere, parental task, and personality. Figure 1 illustrates the typical confounding and the alternative model proposed here.

Gender roles are complex schema which reflect some interaction of biology, personality, social behavior, and social context, as well as the learning that transpires in those contexts. Even in the brief review of the research on sex differences, one can see the confusion caused by using "man" and "woman" to refer to "gender" and "sex." The definition and use of the term "gender," as well as of the terms "masculine" and of "feminine," must be as precise as possible in order to be useful in any ongoing discussion of how men and women—people—relate to one another.[9] I suggest a use that limits the term *gender* (and its representative constituents *masculine* and *feminine*) to attitudes, feelings, and behaviors (features of personality) that may be experienced and expressed by any person, without limiting that expression due to any contiguity of biological sex, parent label, or social sphere; this definition places gender, gender-identity, and gender-role function in the realm of personality.

An example suggesting the need for—and, at the same time, making a case for—this distinction between sex and gender comes from the psychological literature on grief. Bregman and Thiermann (1995) examined written narrative accounts of men and women giving care to dying loved ones. They predicted that male and female caregivers would respond differently to the caregiving and mourning experiences following the adage of one widowed participant, Xenia Rose: "women mourn; men replace" (p. 108). They found no evidence in their study to support conclusions of the presence of sex differences in the grief experiences of the participants. Only one sex difference was in the

study: "Overwhelmingly, women remain the primary caretakers for the sick and the elderly" (p. 109). They conclude:
> [A] host of preconceptions [exist] that written works by men and women will be different. ... In fact, a new set of stereotypes about [men and women has] emerged to overlay, and in some cases, confirm an older set about the natural roles of men and women. ... most of the clichés about gender ... are simply not borne out in our collection of narratives. ... Take, for instance, one of the themes popularized by Carol Gilligan that women are more relational [than men]. ... This perspective is not really new since it is indeed a view very close to a much older view of women as naturally at home in the private sphere of personal, familial relationships. (pp. 106–107)

Reports of these narrators do not support Gilligan's claim; "such stories [of personal dealings with grief] are relational at their core, no matter who tells them" (p. 107).

Gender is not "men" and "women" as social groups; it is clusters of personality traits—thoughts, feelings, and behaviors—that in some primitive way are experienced as analogs of sexual behavior, but are not prescribed by the sex of the actor. This quality of gendered experience could be called *genderality*: the quality or state of being gendered, masculine and feminine. This use of the word "genderality" would be parallel to the use of the word "sexuality" which means
> "the quality or state of being sexual: a: the condition of having sex, b: sexual activity, c: expression of sexual receptivity or interest, esp. when excessive" (*Merriam-Webster's Collegiate Dictionary*, 1993, p. 1074).

Sexuality is marked by physiological, genetic, or hormonal traits while genderality is marked by thoughts, feelings, and behaviors.

Descriptors typically associated with the feminine are: receptive, passive, soft, emotional, expressive, submissive, dark, mysterious, irrational, intuitive, evil, bodily, bloody, earthy, vulnerable, relational, dependent, demurring, acquiescing, etc. (Bem, 1974; Deutsch, 1945; Freud, 1925; Friedan, 1963; Hillman, 1979, 1985; Horney, 1967; Johnson, 1974, 1989a, 1989b, 1991; C. G. Jung, 1931; E. Jung, 1972; Mead, 1949; Monick, 1987, 1991; Ulanov, 1981; von Franz, 1972; Woodman, 1980, 1982, 1985, 1990; Wyly, 1989). These attributes often have been considered descriptive only of women, but are not necessarily.[10]

The masculine has been described as: assertive, autonomous, active, initiating, hard, unemotional, instrumental, dominant, light, obvious, rational, logical, good, mental, spiritual, ideational, strong, autonomous, independent, aggressive, and so forth (Balswick, 1988;

Bem, 1974; Deutsch, 1945; Freud, 1925; Friedan, 1963; Hillman, 1979, 1985; Horney, 1967; Johnson, 1974, 1989a, 1989b, 1991; C. G. Jung, 1931; E. Jung, 1972; Mead, 1949; Monick, 1987, 1991; Ulanov, 1981; von Franz, 1972; Woodman, 1980, 1982, 1985, 1990; Wyly, 1989). These attributes often have been considered descriptive only of men but are not necessarily.[11]

Historically, primary sexual characteristics (i.e., the reproductive organs) have been taken as organizing metaphors of gendered traits: cognitive, affective, and conative traits which seem consistent with these sex traits have been assigned to the categories associated with the biological metaphors. Thus, a shorthand understanding of femininity is suggested by the containing and receptive shape of female genital construction; while masculinity is suggested by the erect and intruding penis. However, these metaphors quickly become confusing and crippling if they are taken literally. Individuals are not simply their bodies (and certainly not merely their sex organs), nor are biological traits the only determinants of most social behaviors. Further, because of the inclination to apply the genital metaphor as a concrete physical reality, it has been considered inappropriate, pathological, and even sinful for members of a given sex to display the characteristics attributed to the other.[12] For example, the argument that only men may be priests is based on an understanding that (a) since the priest represents Jesus in function he must also be like Jesus in body, and (b) since women menstruate they are "unclean" and would "defile" the Sacraments when handling them.[13]

Dinnerstein (1976) stated that the modes of male-female relating have developed over thousands of years, forming a stable complementarity that leaves both members of the dyad immature in part of their personality functioning. She suggested that this arrangement has been mutually convenient, but also mutually debilitating, for women and for men. Men develop maturity in their "feeling or real possession of the status that [their fathers] had in the eyes of the child," while remaining "less adult . . . [in relation to] so powerful a figure as the mother whom [all women] partly become" (p. 86). On the other hand, women are, "in sex, both more nurturing and supportive (i.e., adult) and more dependent and submissive (i.e., childlike) toward the man than he is toward her" (p. 86). "[T]he boy is likely to succeed more completely than the girl at incorporating subjectively the authority of the same-sex parent [his father]; but this authority was at the outset more finite [than his mother's]" (p. 87).

To describe this complementarity according to the terms of the current study, women are mature in their exercise and expression of femininity, and men are mature in their exercise and expression of masculinity. According to Dinnerstein's evaluation, women are able to identify with the procreative and nurturant power of the mother, and to develop a sense of identity that is grounded in that power. They remain infantile in their sense of themselves as individuals who produce goods and ideas for public enrichment. Alternately, men discovered that they were different from mother and identified with the

> worldly competence [of the father, in order to achieve] membership in the wider community where prowess was displayed, enterprise planned, public event organized. ... The eventual adult [male believes] that love for women must be kept in its place, [and] not allowed to interfere with the vital ties between men. (pp. 48–49)

They remain infantile in their capacity for interpersonal nurturance and intimacy.[14]

Dinnerstein (cf. Chodorow, 1978) believes that differential adoption of these gendered behaviors in most western cultures is due to the overwhelming influence exerted on children of both sexes by mother-only parenting practices. Further, she believes that change in male-female complementarity is possible only if more mutual parenting occurs. As a result of both fathers and mothers being intimately involved in child-rearing, men and women and girls and boys will develop identities that are more mutually inclusive of masculine and feminine behaviors, attitudes, and traits. The masculine and feminine, the genderality of persons, must become viewed as human traits rather than traits associated with men and women, respectively. A first step in achieving the humanization and valorization of the traits is to identify and describe them without reference to men and to women, but rather as human qualities and practices.

Summary

Whether one is reading Aristotle (c. 986 BCE) or the description of the construction of Bem's (1974) Sex Role Inventory, one finds that the assumptions about what is masculine and what is feminine remain relatively constant. Even after two waves of feminism and into a third (Friedan, 1989; Steinem, 1991), understandings of these categories of prove resistant to change in the common culture. Women have increased opportunity and social sanction to behave in more "masculine" ways than in the past. Men's expression of "femininity" is still severely limited in almost all areas. There is something about identifying the feminine with woman and the masculine with man that continues to impose itself on human thought and discourse (Gray,

1992; Moir & Jessel, 1991). In fact, it is still common in social settings to hear such statements as, "he's [or, she's] so masculine," "he's effeminate," "she's not feminine enough," or "he's all boy." Since the words, masculine and feminine, and the traits that they describe enjoy such common popular use, it would be wise to operationalize them so that they convey clear and relevant information about human beings.

In order to understand and use the concepts—gender, masculine, and feminine—in helpful and instructive ways, a behavioral and interpersonal description of them is needed. While Bem's (1974) list of gender descriptors is a helpful first step, it does not adequately describe the interpersonal nature nor the exact character of masculine and feminine functions in the social environment. Further, Bem's descriptions are limited because they include only positive attributes, even though many gendered behaviors and attitudes are assigned a negative value, depending on the social context in which they occur and the sex of the actor. The model developed by Benjamin (1974), Structural Analysis of Social Behavior (SASB), provides such descriptions of interpersonal behavior.

Gender and the Structural Analysis of Social Behavior

Structural Analysis of Social Behavior is a model for describing interpersonal behavior developed by Lorna Smith Benjamin (1974) and based on the interpersonal psychology of Sullivan (1953)[15] and the circumplex model of Leary (1957). Sullivan described the human infant as having a primary need for emotional and physical contact with other people. From this understanding Sullivan developed a theory of personality which is fundamentally interpersonal in nature, giving the achievement and maintenance of relationship a central meaning in the life of the person. According to Sullivan, the infant's need and the quality of social interactions with early caregivers that lead to need satisfaction or need frustration significantly shape adult expectations and behaviors.[16]

From outside the field of psychoanalysis, Murray attempted to understand psychoanalytic concepts and to study them empirically. Extending the work of the early psychoanalysts and modifying it by application of the hormonic psychology of McDougall (1908) and the field theory of Lewin (1936), Murray (1938) described personality in terms of physical drives and "psychogenic needs." Building on his theory, Freedman, Leary, Ossorio, and Coffey (1951) and Leary (1957) designed the Interpersonal Circle that became the basis for Benjamin's model.

SASB is a circumplex model of social behavior built along three axes: affiliation, interdependence, and focus. It can be used as a means of digitizing and quantifying complex and multi-channeled interpersonal communication while retaining the wealth of information contained in those communications. The model has been validated using a variety of statistical techniques, giving it the advantage of an empirically rigorous foundation (Benjamin, 1974, 1984).

The SASB model designates behavior along three dimensions. *Focus*, the first dimension, may be directed toward Self, Other or Introject (i.e., the internalized sense of self as subject and object). These objects of focus are modeled as three separate two-axis planes, each of which contains the other two dimensions: Affiliation on the horizontal axis, and Interdependence on the vertical (see Figure 2).

In an interpersonal encounter, when one person's communication attends to the other person's experience, these behaviors are transitive and are described by the model as "focus on other." When one person's communication focuses on his or her own experience, the these behaviors are intransitive and are described by the model as "focus on self." When, in an interpersonal communication, one person is orienting the attention to an inner psychic representation of the self, the behavior is introspective and is described as "focus on introject."

Benjamin (1974) named the second dimension of interpersonal behavior *Interdependence*, referring to the levels of "freedom from" or "dependence on" expressed by the communication; these levels range from free to controlling. The third dimension is called *Affiliation*, referring to the levels of connection or disconnection existing between the members of the dyad; these levels range from hostile to loving.

In the cluster version of the model (which represents intermediate complexity and elaboration) there are eight points on each of three planes: two points representing opposing expressions of interdependence, two representing opposing expressions of affiliation, and four representing intermediate combinations of interdependence and affiliation. This model allows for identification of individual "complete thoughts" and "psychologically meaningful interactions" (Benjamin,

Gender: Feminine and Masculine Defined 45

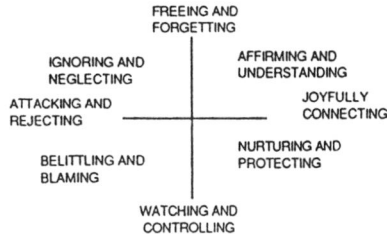

FOCUS ON OTHER

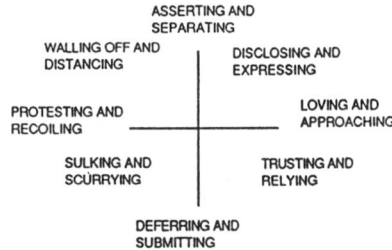

FOCUS ON SELF

```
                    SPONTANEOUS SELF
       DAYDREAMING AND      |    SELF-ACCEPTING
       NEGLECTING SELF      |    AND EXPLORING
                            |
SELF-REJECTING              |         SELF-LOVING AND
AND DESTROYING  ————————————|————————  CHERISHING
                            |
        SELF-INDICTING      |    SELF-NOURISHING
        AND OPPRESSING      |    AND ENHANCING
                            |
                    SELF-MONITORING
                    AND RESTRAINING
```

FOCUS ON INTROJECT

Figure 2. Cluster version of the SASB model. From "Use ot the SASB dimensional model to develop treatment plans for personality disorders. I Narcissism," L. S. Benjamin, 1987a, *Journal of Personality Disorders, 1*, 43-70. Copyright, 1987, The Guilford Press. Reprinted with permission.

Foster, Giat-Roberto, & Estroff, 1986). These elements may be coded for content and process. Content coding attends to the verbal content, while process coding attends to such things as voice tone, posture, eye contact, role relationships, those things which communicate affective and nonverbal information. These data are often subtle, requiring careful attention to nuance.[17]

Several corollary behaviors become available for examination. Naturally occurring social behavior is often complicated. At times, it is likely to communicate more than one message simultaneously: This is a *Complex Message*. SASB allows identification of these simultaneous messages. For example, a person might say, "I want to be with you" (Disclosing and Expressing), while reaching out and taking the other's hand (Loving and Approaching). Thus, the behavior communicates both self-disclosure and active love of the other and requires both codes.

Complementarity exists in an interaction when one person focuses primarily on the other and that other focuses primarily on the self in ways that exhibit comparable amounts of affiliation and interdependence. For example, Person A demonstrates Nurturing and Protecting behavior while Person B exhibits Trusting and Relying behavior. Maximal stability occurs when social interactions are consistently complementary. Consistent patterns of complementary interactions characterize complementary relationships, in which the interactions are hierarchical, in that one person is focused on the other (i.e., parent-like) while the other is focused on the self (i.e., child-like), with little freedom to switch roles.

Opposition occurs when behaviors occur on the same Focus surface at positions 180 degrees apart. For example, Freeing and Forgetting is in opposition to Watching and Controlling. If such opposing behaviors occur together in one Complex Communication from one communicator they are called a Simultaneous Opposite. Benjamin (1979) suggested that a double-bind is a particular Simultaneous Opposite that "exists when verbal and/or nonverbal communications [of one member of the dyad] involve opposite points on the Other surface [plane]" (p. 15), thus, expressing inherent contradiction. According to Rotzien and Vande Kemp (1989a), this construction would form one Double Bind Element (DBE) of a Double Bind Communication Component (DBCC). In order to complete the DBCC, the DBE initiating component must be succeeded by a perpetuating response that contains a Complementary Simultaneous Opposite, thus accepting the interaction as initiated. Rotzien and Vande Kemp gave an example of a double bind: an initiating DBE of Nurturing and Protecting and

Ignoring and Neglecting followed by a perpetuating DBE of Trusting and Relying and Walling Off and Distancing.

The work of Rotzien and Vande Kemp (1989b) suggest that SASB provides a means to explore complex human communications, such as the double bind, in a way that honors both the investigators' need for a naturalistic systems approach to the object of study and their need for an empirical foundation and results. One such set of complex interactions is the communication of gender, that is, beliefs, behaviors, and feelings that communicate masculinity and/or femininity.

Identifying Gender Using the SASB

Previously, I defined "gender" as "features of the human personality that may be experienced and expressed by any human person, regardless of biological sexual identity, parental role, or attendant social sphere." The list of descriptors (see Table 3) created and validated by Bem (1974) can be translated into identifiable gendered social behaviors by applying SASB. By this means, generality will become available for more rigorous study. The difficult, but critical, task of identifying what women and men actually do in their relationships and what they could do, rather than what they should do, becomes possible.

Using SASB, Berlin and Johnson (1989) have demonstrated this approach by identifying the presence of autonomy within an affiliative realm, behaviors which, traditionally, have been considered feminine. Traditionally, men should behave in a masculine way, that is, to act aggressively and autonomously; women should behave in a feminine way, that is, to be submissive, receptive, and selfless. However, the selfless, responsive, and submissive posture of women vis-à-vis the men and children to whom they related could not be truly selfless because of the high level of economic and emotional dependency that women experienced. The satisfaction of their real emotional and physical needs was dependent on the circumstances of the relationships. Thus, women's behaviors necessarily contained complex messages of friendly and hostile control of men and children (Focus on Other) as well as friendly and hostile control of themselves (Focus on Self). Women were not autonomous, not because they were warmly bonded to others, but because they were dependent on others.

According to Berlin and Johnson (1989), related autonomy is represented by the behaviors described on the upper right side of each model surface: Affirming and Understanding, Loving and Approaching, Disclosing and Expressing, Joyfully Connecting, Self-Accepting and Exploring, and Self-Loving and Cherishing. These behaviors are consistent with findings of recent research describing "women's ways" and "women's voice" as having a moral intent to maintain interpersonal connection without denying that women function autonomously as well. The approach taken by Berlin and Johnson has the further benefit of maintaining a positive understanding of and value for autonomy. Using SASB to describe and identify autonomy within connection is a method that may be applied heuristically to identify a variety of gendered traits and functions. The masculine and feminine items of the Bem (1974) Sex Role Inventory can be described in general behavioral categories on the SASB model surfaces, according to the ordinary meanings of the terms used; the results of this interpolation appear in Tables 4 and 5.

Table 4. Comparison BSRI Gender Items and SASB Social Behaviors: Feminine Descriptors

Gender	Social behavior
childlike	FOCUS ON SELF surface
affectionate, cheerful	DISCLOSE
compassionate	DISCLOSE, REACTIVE LOVE
sympathetic	REACTIVE LOVE
flatterable, gullible, yielding	TRUST, SUBMIT
gentle, shy, soft spoken	TRUST, SUBMIT, SELF-CONTROL
soothe hurt feelings	AFFIRM, PROTECT, REACTIVE LOVE
sensitive to others' needs	FOCUS ON OTHERS
warm	AFFIRM, DISCLOSE
loyal	AFFIRM, TRUST
tender	AFFIRM, REACTIVE LOVE
understanding	AFFIRM
loves children	AFFIRM, LOVE, PROTECT
no harsh language	not ATTACK, not BLAME

Note. BSRI = Bem Sex Role Inventory; SASB = Structural Analysis of Social Behavior.

Table 5. Comparison BSRI Gender Items and SASB Social Behaviors: Masculine Descriptors

Gender	Social behavior
takes risks, decisive, dominant	CONTROL, PROTECT, DISCLOSE
athletic	CONTROL, ATTACK, PROTECT SEPARATE, RECOIL, WALL OFF
aggressive, competitive	CONTROL, ATTACK, SEPARATE
forceful	CONTROL, WALL OFF, SEPARATE
ambitious, analytical, strong personality	CONTROL, SEPARATE, DISCLOSE
defends own beliefs	DISCLOSE, SEPARATE
individualistic,	IGNORE, SEPARATE, DISCLOSE
leader, leadership ability	CONTROL, AFFIRM, DISCLOSE
self-reliant	DISCLOSE, SEPARATE
self-sufficient	DISCLOSE SEPARATE
independent	SEPARATE
assertive	SEPARATE, DISCLOSE
takes a stand	DISCLOSE

Note. BSRI = Bem Sex Role Inventory; SASB = Structural Analysis of Social Behavior.

The feminine descriptors are located about equally on the Focus on Self and Focus on Other surfaces, and they fall almost exclusively on the Friendly Connected side of both surfaces. Masculine descriptors are located about equally on the Focus on Self and Focus on Other surfaces, and they are about equally divided between Friendly Control, Friendly Autonomy, and Hostile Autonomy. A view of masculinity, aided by the SASB model, highlights the cultural association of masculinity with hostility. Although men are often the perpetrators of violence, they are certainly not the only perpetrators, women also may be violent. This issue of who commits violence underscores the difference between sex (maleness and femaleness) and gender (masculinity and femininity). In contrast to hostility which is generally thought of as unacceptable interpersonal behavior, connection (the feminine counterpart) is portrayed by Benjamin as positively valued. However, connectedness may be unacceptable, unwanted, and unhelpful at times.

Certainly, not all social behavior is gendered behavior; however, all gendered behavior is in some fundamental way social. Since masculine behavior has been generally defined as independent, aggressive, and dominant while feminine behavior has been described as dependent, meek, and submissive, these definitions can be used heuristically to identify gendered behavior in terms of the descriptions of the interpersonal behaviors displayed on the SASB model surfaces. This interpolation yields an identification of gendered behaviors as shown in Figure 3. On the Focus on Other surface behavior generally considered masculine is predominantly separating and disaffiliating, while behavior generally considered feminine is predominantly affiliating and depending. On the Focus on Self surface, masculine behavior is also predominantly separating and disaffiliating with slightly more affiliation and slightly less dependence expressed, as compared to masculinity on the Focus on Other surface. Feminine behavior is predominantly affiliating and depending with slightly less affiliation and more independence expressed, when compared to femininity on the Focus on Other surface. In some instances on the model surfaces masculine and feminine social behaviors appear to be opposites. Heuristically, since complementary behavior is the most stable, it is highly likely that gendered behaviors, when expressed interpersonally, will be complementary; however, this is not to say that the feminine is the opposite of masculine on a bipolar continuum, nor that feminine and masculine are mutually exclusive, complementary realms of behavior, nor that men will exhibit the masculine behaviors that complement the feminine behaviors of women. Future study of genderality with the SASB may be facilitated by using the most elaborated model surfaces since it provides the most behavioral specificity.[18]

A caution is needed at this point: it is critical to remember that these designations of gendered behavior refer to attributes of personality without regard to individual persons' biological sex. Men and women may exhibit both feminine and masculine traits. The caution is necessary because the behaviors are not neutrally valued in western culture; positive value is assigned to some behaviors while negative value is assigned to others. Further, positive and negative value may be assigned to gendered traits differentially, depending on (a) the sex of the actor, (b) the characteristics of the person being acted upon, and (c) the social context in which the action occurs. This caution will become critical in the later discussions of gender as related to shame and power.

Gender: Feminine and Masculine Defined 51

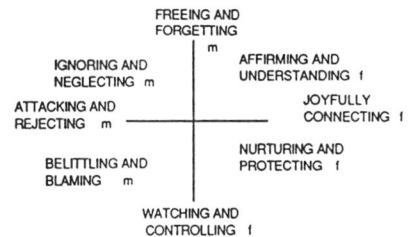

FOCUS ON OTHER

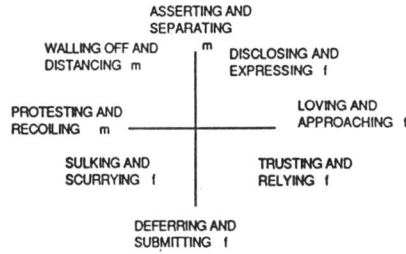

FOCUS ON SELF

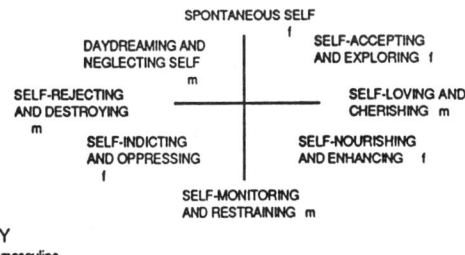

KEY
m = masculine
f = feminine

FOCUS ON INTROJECT

Figure 3. Cluster version of the SASB Model, with masculine and feminine social behaviors designated.

Conclusion: Values and Gender

Historically, from the advent of the Greco-Roman era, western culture has placed a higher value on masculine characteristics and has devalued and denigrated feminine traits (de Beauvoir, 1952; Dinnerstein, 1976; Doyle & Paludi, 1985; Friedan, 1963; Johnson, 1974; Ranke-Heinemann, 1990; Woodman, 1980). In their extreme forms the feminine has been associated (and confused with) the vulnerability of the vanquished and the masculine with the invincibility of the conqueror.[19] Because of these experienced extremes, feelings of shame have come to be associated with "femininity."

Psychological and sociological understandings of "masculine" and "feminine" become highly significant,[20] especially as their impact on the development of individual identity and interpersonal function comes under scrutiny. Precision in the use of the terms "gender", "masculine", and "feminine", keeping them as free as possible from confounds, is critical to an accurate understanding of how shame has become a prevalent feature of women's and men's reactions to the expression of feminine aspects of human personality. When individuals are rewarded or punished in ways that lead them experience shame for being "feminine," valuable and normal parts of human personality become unavailable for the negotiation of human experiences and relationships. In this case it is not simply women's voice, but rather the voicing of "feminine" experience by women *and* men that is silenced.

I believe that the presence of "feminine strivings" (Kaplan, 1991)— that is, the desire of human beings to express the feminine (soft, dependent, submissive) parts of the self—is experienced as shameful by men and boys because it is Man (the collective archetype of maleness in men) experiencing the self as negated, as "not Man" (Chodorow, 1978; Dinnerstein, 1976; Kaplan, 1991, Lynn, 1969). Experiencing this self-annihilation results in feelings of shame and a desire to escape annihilation (Lewis, 1971; Nathanson, 1987, 1992). Then, in order to ward off the shame, the feminine strivings are projected onto women— that is, only women are "feminine." By means of projective identification[21] the boy or man puts his femininity, as well as his feelings of shame at having it, into the significant women in his relational sphere so that he does not have to continue being unmanned. For example, a parishioner once told his pastor in all seriousness that he would starve to death if his wife did not leave prepared food for him while she was out of town. It was inconceivable to this man that he could express "feminine" nurturant behavior for or toward himself: he has successfully projected all such nurturance into his wife, and she had enacted it for him for 47 years.

Or, take for instance, the cliché, but often all too real, response of a sexual assailant "she asked for it" regarding a woman's role in "causing" his sexual assault; the man has forcibly projected his feminine arousal and desire into the woman's identity, while retaining his hatred and anger toward his disowned femininity.

A third example is the woman who prohibits her husband's help with child care because he is "incompetent" at the tasks; she projects her own narrative of masculine incompetence into him such that he becomes bumbling and mildly dangerous to the child.

A final example is of a woman whose husband became disabled for a period of months. Her initial response was assertive action to get treatment for him and to visit him in the hospital. However, when it became necessary to provide simple daily care such as shampooing his hair or fixing his meals, she invited her mother-in-law to come help and proceeded to immerse herself in work 12 and 14 hours each day. She experienced him and his disability as overwhelmingly needy (projecting "feminine" helplessness into him), and fled from his received, her disowned vulnerability.

As women have become more active in public life (traditionally male-dominated, and controlled by the valuing of masculinity) there has been increasing pressure on women to suppress or deny feminine behaviors, feelings and attitudes.[22] This form of personality functioning in women has been called "animus-identification" (Jung, 1931) or "male-identification" (Deutsch, 1945; Freud, 1925; Horney, 1967). One must wonder: if men rid themselves of feelings of shame at their femininity by the use of projective identification in their relations with women, and if women as well increasingly feel the need to rid themselves of these same shameful attributes, who will express femininity for humankind?[23] One possibility is that those groups who constitute the underclasses, including two-thirds-world men and women, homosexual women and men, and male and female prostitutes, will carry both positive and negative feminine traits, as they already carry responsibility for the accomplishment of certain unpleasant and repetitive tasks that are needed to maintain culture, such as illicit sex, housework, yard care, child care, food production, and hard or dangerous physical labor. Will they also bear the consequent shame for behaving in disapproved and disavowed ways?

In the next chapter I will discuss the philosophical and theological foundations that lead to the shaming of feminine behaviors and attitudes.

Chapter 3.
A Brief History of Sex and Gender

"Woman! You are the gateway of the devil. You persuaded him who the devil dared not attack directly. Because of you the son of God had to die. You should always go dressed in mourning and in rags."
Tertullian (cited in de Beauvoir)

"Among all savage beasts none is found so harmful as woman."
St. John Chrysostom (cited in de Beauvoir)

Even though women's roles have been undergoing rapid, intense, and extensive change during the last century, roles for women in previous centuries were largely limited to those that could be performed at or near home where children were being nourished and tended, food was raised and gathered, and households were managed. Women's work was often limited to tasks that required more fine motor skill and less brute strength than did tasks assigned to men. Contiguous with the gendered practices necessitated by nonindustrial agriculture and manufacturing, there arose a body of thought about women and women's roles which fostered limiting women to the domestic sphere and which assigned differential value to women and men as well as to their work. A brief historical review of thought regarding sex and gender will highlight sources of shame that have come to be associated with femininity and femaleness.

Early Philosophy, Theology, and Biological Determinism

Plato and early Jewish and Christian theologians agreed that to be a woman was not good (de Beauvoir, 1952; Ranke-Heinemann, 1990). Plato expressed gratitude and relief that he was born male, not female. Jewish rabbis prayed "Thank God I am not a woman." Without

establishing an empirical basis for his assignations, Aristotle, in his *Metaphysics*, asserted these polarities:
    male-limited-odd-one-right-square-at rest-straight-light-good;
and
    female-unlimited-even-plurality-left-oblong-moving-curved-darkness-evil (cited in Maclean, 1980, pp. 2–3).

The Apostle Paul has been interpreted as teaching that women were to be in subjugation to men because Eve, the woman, was responsible for the Fall (I Timothy 2:9–15). The Christian gnostics taught that good women who attempted the spiritual disciplines, if they succeeded in the enterprise, would be changed into men in order to receive their spiritual reward (Brown, 1988; Clark, 1989; Kelsey & Kelsey, 1986; Lawrence, 1989; Maclean, 1980; Pagels, 1979, 1988; Ranke-Heinemann, 1990).

Gnosticism

Within Christianity gnosticism was a major challenge to the early church during its formative period in the first century (Brown, 1988; Clark, 1989; Culianu, 1987; Durant, 1926; Goodwin, 1981; Perkins, 1987; Quispel, 1987; Ranke-Heinemann, 1990). Two basic tenets of gnosticism are relevant to the current discussion of gender and its cultural appraisal. The first tenet is dualism: The material world is set over against the spiritual. According to gnostic teaching, the material world was created by God's own created spirits in rebellion against a wholly spiritual God. True spirit (the Good and God) is in conflict with evil matter; the goal of human spirituality is to escape from matter and the body which is the spirit's prison. Having been influenced by gnostic thought, Augustine saw relations with women (even for husbands with wives) as a serious impediment to the fulfillment of the spiritual life because such relations would lead to concupiscence (that is, to lust and sexual intercourse). In splitting the world into the spiritual and the material, gnostics split off sexed and gendered experience from the rest of human experience which prepared the way for the devaluation of the feminine.

The second tenet is devaluation of the material world which led gnostics to take one of two attitudes toward sexuality. Either they practiced a severe asceticism which included celibacy and even castration, or they behaved licentiously. The devaluation of sex and the body extended to include the object of men's sexual behavior: woman. Two related Christian heresies influenced the formulation of the church's teaching about the body and materiality: Docetism taught that

Jesus was not really human, but only appeared human (an affirmation of his divinity and a denial of his embodied humanity); and Arianism taught that Jesus was not the same substance as God, only the best created being (an affirmation of his material human body and a denial of his divinity). In its early credal formulations the church attacked the gnostic rejection of the body. The Council of Nicea declared the value of the body in declaring Christ at once divine and human, and in affirming the bodily resurrection; however, the rise of ascetic practices among Christians undermined their esteem for the body and for women (Brown, 1988; Clark, 1989; Ranke-Heinemann, 1990).

During this period there were practical reasons that led both women and men to eschew the body and sexual behavior; however, the result has been a lasting legacy of despising materiality, sexuality, and femininity. Throughout early Christian history, woman and femininity continued to be associated with nature, dirt, and evil. For Christian men, women with their attendant sexuality were viewed as "occasions for sin."[1] Simultaneously, women who chose ordinary lives of sexual activity and its consequent, childbirth, were vilified; other women, who chose to repudiate their "natural" desires and undertake religious life, were revered. For Christian women marriage, child-bearing, and child-rearing came to be viewed as impediments to the spiritual life. For both women and men, virginity came to be viewed as the highest good. Renunciation of sexual activity and childbearing may have improved women's lives substantially, giving them more status and more freedom than was available outside Christianity. However, in so doing women adopted an attitude of contempt toward nature, the body, and the feminine that necessarily led also to self-contempt (Brown, 1988; Clark, 1989; Ranke-Heinemann, 1990).

The Renaissance and the Enlightenment

During the Renaissance and the Enlightenment, gnostic sects such as Jansenism reemerged periodically to threaten the church from within, albeit at its margins (Culianu, 1987; Perkins, 1987; Quispel, 1987; Ranke-Heinemann, 1990). An example from Protestantism is the Puritan movement, with its emphasis on denial, duty, religious obligation, and abstemiousness. Puritanism portrayed God as a severe masculine agent, whose attitude toward creation and human beings was aggressively condemning and punitive. Puritans were extreme in their restrictions of women's roles as well as in their restrictions on sexual behavior. According to Hymowitz and Weissman (1978), an abiding fear of witchcraft—"a morbid preoccupation with the devilish powers of women" (p. 17)—caused the Puritans to prosecute and to kill many women during the 1600s (See de Beauvoir, 1952; Ranke-Heinemann, 1990).[2]

Increasingly secular Enlightenment philosophies of the 18th century focused on taming the wildness and evilness of nature, including the human passions. Even though many adherents of the movement rejected religious dogma and traditional social and political ideas, their focus on rationalism reinforced prior religious attitudes of contempt for the body, women, and the feminine. During this period women were still associated with Nature, with Eros and with the passions because of their role in childbirth, while men were associated with Logos (the mind-spirit) because of their pursuit of intellectual life. As wealthy, aristocratic men received more education, they gained more control over women and children in order to protect them and to advance the salvation and perfection of the world (Cushman, 1990; de Beauvoir, 1952; Luepnitz, 1988; Maclean, 1980; Ranke-Heinemann, 1990).

As the split between the sacred and the secular grew, the split between the material and the mental grew as well. The mind-body dualism of gnosticism found a new home in scientific materialism. However, science redefined the relationship between mind and matter. Unlike religion, which had exercised mind over matter in order to escape from the material world into the spiritual world, science exercised mind over matter in order to describe, to know, to control, and to exploit nature for the benefit of humankind (de Beauvoir, 1952; Cushman, 1990; Maclean, 1980).[3]

However, somewhat later a strange reversal occurred. In *More Work for Mother*, Cowan (1989) chronicles changes in women's work that occurred as a result of industrialization. Material life became increasingly separated from mental life for those engaged in the manufacture of goods; more work became less mentally engaging and less emotionally satisfying; and productivity was increasingly taken out of the home. The shift that was occurring in the location of production from the home or farm to the factory occasioned a split between public life and private life that left women at home with children, other caregiving adults, and aging or disabled family members. The rise of the middle-class also provided more leisure for many women at home who stopped producing goods and became providers of emotional care and direct body care for their families (See Hymowitz & Weissman, 1978).

Men found that industrialization solved some problems while creating others. Society was not becoming perfect, as had been hoped. In the lives of men, conquest of natural forces was replaced by competition with each other in industry and commerce for jobs and wages. The workplace was becoming interpersonal, and the aggression and physical strength which once served to catch and kill food or to prepare the land for cultivation of food became less relevant and more threatening to economic survival. As men continued to experience the world of work as dangerous, they came to regard the home as a haven. Women and the homes they made became the containers of and the antidotes for the frustration and aggression that arose in men's work experiences (de Beauvoir, 1952; Cowan, 1989; Hymowitz & Weissman, 1978; Kimmel, 1987; Mitchell, 1971; Pleck, 1981).

As the workplace became associated with aggression, competition, and men, the home became associated with peace, cooperation, and women. Because of the bifurcation of emotions such that comfort occurred at home and aggression occurred at work, many members of society, at least in the United States and England, concluded that women, who maintained peace-filled homes, must be morally superior to men; women displayed character that was "gentler, more virtuous, more fair-minded, and more concerned for the general welfare than men" (Hymowitz & Weissman, 1978, p. 218) and was lacking in "'low' and 'animalistic' sexual drives [lust] and urges" (p. 219).[4] Upperclass female reformers in the United States joined the quest to perfect nature by reforming the slums, tenements, and barrooms.

Even as American women were succeeding in attempts to alleviate the ill effects of rapid industrialization and situational overpopulation, they were still considered incompetent to vote, to hold public office, or to speak in church or other public gatherings. According to law married women held no property, could not sit on a jury, and could not sue in court. Further, women were prohibited from participation in a variety of political processes (Hymowitz & Weissman, 1978). Women's "moral superiority" did not translate into general participation in public and political life.

In summary, throughout most of the history of western civilization, femininity was concretely associated with bodily femaleness. Women were viewed for several centuries as inferior and dangerous in many aspects of their nature and behavior. At the beginning of the 19th century, philosophers, theologians, and physicians viewed women as physically and morally weaker and inferior when compared to men, as evidenced by their desire to bear children, by their uncleanness in menstruation, and by their higher and earlier death rate (Maclean, 1980; Ranke-Heinemann, 1990). At the time Freud undertook his work, women were described by physicians throughout Europe as more susceptible to disease, more likely to die at an early age, and as the primary sufferers of nervous disorders such as hysteria (Horney, 1967;

Mitchell, 1971, 1974). Much of what was taught about women in the 19th and early 20th centuries was from the growing field of medicine and from the newly emerging disciplines of psychiatry and neurology. Sigmund Freud was one of the foremost thinkers and teachers to emerge in these fields in the late 1800s.

Freud and Freudians

It has become common to reject Freud's conceptions of femininity and his theories of its development (see Chodorow, 1978; Gilligan, 1982; Horney, 1967; Mitchell, 1974). His descriptions of the qualities of women and femininity were in keeping with the values and understandings of his time and culture. However, the reasons Freud gave to explain the observed differences were unique (Freud, 1905, 1914, 1925, 1931, 1933; see Horney, 1967; Kaplan, 1991; Mitchell, 1974). He stated that women were weaker than men, passive, and generally masochistic in their human relations because they had discovered as little girls that they and their mothers had no penises. Freud believed that little girls coveted the penis, and could never get over not having one. This disappointment caused them to hate their mothers and to envy[5] and covet their fathers. Freud believed that they consoled themselves with getting babies as substitute penises. One must conclude that Freud defined woman as "not man" and feminine as "not masculine," and that both of these definitions were predicated on the singularly incomplete observation of "no penis." While Descartes declared "I think, therefore I am", Freud seems to have thought: She has no penis, therefore she is not.

Followers of Freud attempted to support his theories. Anna Freud (1945) observed children and adolescents in order to verify her father's conceptions of the superego and its development. She attempted to demonstrate the existence of penis envy and its resulting interference of moral development in women (Chesler, 1972; Chodorow, 1974; Freud, 1945; Mitchell, 1974). Karl Abraham (cited in Kaplan, 1991) elaborated Freud's thought through the analysis of a 3 year-old girl who played hide-and-seek with her daddy's cigars, citing this incident as proof that girls experienced castration anxiety and penis envy. However, feminists assert that the entire analysis is predicated on males' fear of castration as projected onto the girl (Kaplan, 1991); a parallel conclusion would be that a boy who played with mud in a bucket envied the womb.

Helene Deutsch (1945), in analyzing adult women, expanded and refined Freud's theories on masochism and femininity. Deutsch, even more than Freud, believed that women were oriented toward masochistic human relations due to the "traumatic" quality of adult female sexual experience. The girl's and woman's experience of the pain and bloodiness and danger of intercourse and childbirth predisposed, or even predetermined, that she must become masochistic in her human relations. Deutsch appeared to be saying that to be a woman is always to be a victim, due to her biological nature of being the one who bleeds and of being the one who is penetrated during intercourse (See Horney, 1967; Kaplan, 1991).

Horney (1967) was dissatisfied with the conceptions of penis envy and masochism as Freud, Abraham, and Deutsch described them. Horney believed, rather, that the personality of women was organized primarily around the young girl's discovery of the vagina and her growing awareness that her sense of self rested in her capacity to give birth to children. Horney acknowledged that little girls, upon discovering that little boys have penises and little girls do not, did experience some worry that their penises had been removed. However, she insisted that little girls quickly develop an increasingly accurate sense of their own physicality (the presence of the vagina) which shaped their sense of themselves and their relations with those around them. The primary change in Horney's conception as compared to Freud's was in her definition of "woman" as something in itself, rather than as "not man."

However, Horney's definition of woman and the feminine reflected a strong association between the woman's sense of self and her biology and physiology; woman's sense of her self relies on her acceptance of the control her body exerts on her mental life. On the other hand, Horney's (and Freud's) understanding of the male and masculinity emphasized achievement of a mental life in order to overcome biology; man's sense of self relies on his exercise of reason to control the body. That is, for Horney and for Freud, man becomes Man because his biological predicament forces him beyond his penis to the use of his mind (in the development of his moral sense) as defining his nature; whereas, woman becomes Woman by accepting her uterus and its fruit and giving up intellectual striving.[6]

Challenges to Freud

Several of Freud's most promising protégés separated from him over differences of opinion regarding elements of his theory. They wanted him to modify his understanding of drives in order to accommodate various hypotheses that nonbiological drives or motives influenced the development of the human organism. Adler, Ferenczi, Rank, and Jung were among the students of Freud who challenged his overemphasis on biological determinism.

Adler, Ferenczi, and Rank. Adler believed that psychosocial relations, especially power relations, had a much stronger influence on human personality than Freud's theories allowed. In keeping with the emphasis on the psychosocial development of personality, Adler gave less attention to the libidinal forces at work in the child and more attention to the family's role (including the role of siblings) on training the child in character values (Ansbacher & Ansbacher, 1956). Adler (1910/1956) described the development of self as guided by a "subjective feeling of inferiority" and a consequent desire for superiority, both being grounded in an unconscious defense against femininity. Adler defined the feminine as weak, submissive, inhibited, deficient, cowardly, obedient, shy, masochistic and poor. His definition of the feminine was derived from his observations regarding the child's experience vis-à-vis the parents. In relation to them, the child experienced himself or herself as submissive and dependent, while experiencing wishes and actions of striving for independence and self-will. The child came to associate strength with the stronger parent (thought to be the father). "The renunciation of masculinity, however, appears to the child synonymous with femininity" (Adler, 1910/1956, p. 47). Adler does not clarify how weakness and submissiveness came to be associated with the "feminine-not male" construct in the child's mind; one might conclude that the association depended on the child's observation that, in the family, the father was assigned higher status and value than the mother and that the lesser value assigned to femininity "holds . . . also for the greater part of our culture. Thus a wide area of originally childish value judgments is given" (p. 47). It seems that a preferable conclusion, which remains closer to the child's experience, would be that independence and will are construed mentally by the child as "parent-not child." However, for Adler, the construction was "feminine-not male," and, in his theory, subsequent psychoemotional maturation of the child was directed against femininity/inferiority. Adler concluded that "[t]his inner disunion in the child is the prototype and foundation of the most important psychological phenomena, especially neurosis, the splitting of consciousness" (p. 47) and sets the starting point of the "masculine protest" whereby

> [u]ncertainty regarding our own ability arouses doubt and inaugurates vacillation between the feminine tendencies of anxiety and related

phenomena and the masculine tendencies of aggression and compulsion phenomena. ... feminine traits [are] carefully hidden by hypertrophied masculine efforts. ... such as overcompensation, because the feminine tendency is evaluated negatively and is retained only in sublimated form for external advantage. (p. 48)

In Adler's thought, as in Freud's, the feminine continued to be viewed as "not masculine" and as subjugated to the other. A more neutral or positive view of the parent-child relationship (a view that may not have been warranted by social realities if Freud's Seduction Theory was in fact true) might have recognized connection or relatedness (a hallmark of femininity) as a valuable capacity.

Ferenczi and Rank sought to address the role of relatedness in psychoanalytic thought and practice. According to de Forest (1954) Ferenczi also departed from Freud in significant ways by shifting his theoretical emphasis to the relational nature of the therapeutic relationship, likening it to that of the mother and infant. Here is an early recognition of the importance of relatedness to the creation of a healthy sense of self, without giving explicit attention to gender.

Jung and gender. Jung's critique centered on Freud's over-reliance on biological and external experience for descriptions of psychological events. Jung countered that inner mental images gathered from the culture (the Archetypes), as well as from personal experience, had a powerful organizing influence on the mental and emotional experience of the individual. He identified and described two contrasexual intrapsychic elements (the anima in men and the animus in women) which are images of the feminine and the masculine formed in the personal unconscious and shaped by the individual's direct experiences of important female and male figures in his or her environment as well as by traits from the Archetypal Anima and Animus coming from the collective unconscious. He suggested that individuation (his term for healthy adult development of self) consisted in the integration of these idiosycratic and collective aspects of the self into the conscious personality of the individual.

While he uniquely highlighted the feminine, Jung described ego function in terms of male values and behaviors—that is, independent and instrumental behavior in public settings concretely related to biological sex. His descriptions of feminine behavior imply negative value. When he speaks of a man incorporating his "anima" into consciousness he means that a man will know and recognize his tendencies to express negative affect like vexation and irritability:

"nervous breakdowns in the forties are a very common occurrence . . . what is left over is an effeminate man" (Jung, 1933/1971, p. 16). When he speaks of a woman incorporating her "animus" he means that "the wife then dons the trousers and open a little shop where [the husband] perhaps performs the duties of a handyman" (p. 16) or that she may develop

an uncommonly masculine tough-mindedness which thrusts the feelings and the heart aside. Very often these changes are accompanied by all sorts of catastrophes in the marriage, for it is not hard to imagine what will happen when the husband discovers his tender feelings and the wife her sharpness of mind" (p. 16).

These challenges to Freud have had an impact on conceptions of sexuality and gender. Each of them, though having different focal points, suggested that the individual's experience was shaped in significant ways by the social and cultural setting in which he or she lived. They described a process of gender identity formation that was social and interpersonal. It is significant that Adler turned his attention to the role of social—and, in particular, family—influence, to the fear of inferiority, and its consequent of striving for superiority; and that Ferenczi and Rank developed a deep understanding of and appreciation for the importance of relatedness to mental health. It is also important that Jung developed a largely different model of the self that defined maturity as the incorporation of masculine and feminine attributes into the consciousness of both men and women.

Post-Jungians and gender. Emma Jung (1972) (Carl's wife and also an analyst) and Marie-Louise von Franz (1972) (a student and analysand of Carl) continued Jung's work developing further the concepts of "animus" and "anima." Von Franz explored and elaborated the concept of the feminine, especially as anima (the feminine aspect of the male personality). E. Jung was responsible for more elaborated descriptions of the animus as the masculine aspect of the female personality. Central to the Jungian understanding of masculinity is its rational and penetrating capacities, exemplified by intellect; central to the Jungian understanding of femininity is its relating and receiving capacities, exemplified by feeling. With each of these constructs Jung was attempting to describe intrapsychic realities that were features of the personality expressed in interpersonal relations through certain behaviors and attitudes. Their thinking reflected a contextual reality of the era: Society determined gendered behavior in such a way that women only receive, and men only penetrate. Though the cocnepts were limited, they encompassed more androgynous possibilities.

Several neo-Jungians have continued to develop Jung's concepts of "anima" and "animus" and their relation to the ego. Hillman (1975, 1979, 1985), in distinguishing between soul and spirit, refers to the feminine and the masculine. The soul is associated with the feminine: with night dreams, impressions, imagination, madness, immanence, death, vulnerability, suffering, blood, guts, and depth. Masculine is associated with the spirit: with visions, miracles, intellect, clarity, transcendence, quickening, purity, rules, light, order, and heights.

Woodman (1980, 1982, 1985, 1990) and Johnson (1974, 1976, 1983, 1987, 1989a, 1989b, 1990, 1991) have described the gender development of men and women. The most useful attempt has been Woodman's description of the "feminine ego", the conscious part of the woman's personality that is "feminine" because it is woman's. This construction also conflates biology and personality to some extent. Generally, the tendency to equate femininity as femaleness is objectionable, but in this case the positive valuing of all parts of the woman's conscious self-experience (even the parts of experience that have typically been called "masculine") is a helpful development. For example, if a woman is behaving in an instrumental way, she is being womanly because it is a woman doing the behavior. The former alternative in analytic commentary was to describe instrumental activity in the woman as manly, and then negatively evaluate the activity as against her nature because it somehow made her less suited for her prescribed social role. In treatment this evaluation elicited feelings of guilt and shame rather than rehabilitation and growth. Singer (1972), another neo-Jungian, has stated that androgyny is the goal of individuation and defines "androgyny" as the capacity of the conscious ego to choose responses that are culturally labeled "masculine" or "feminine" according to the need of a given situation rather than according to societal prescriptions for men or for women. This conceptualization is similar to Bem's (1974).[7]

Cultural Anthropology and Sociology

In the late 19th and early 20th centuries anthropology and sociology were emerging as empirical disciplines. They were primarily ethological in their method, providing descriptions of social behavior without giving attention to how and why behavior occurred as it did in a society or culture. Thus, many sex-typed behaviors that were described by researchers in these disciplines at this time ought not to have been treated prescriptively as they were routinely in the middle 1900s (Friedan, 1963; Mead, 1949).

Margaret Mead was a cultural anthropologist, educated in the 1920s, whose observations of many tribal and ethnic groups led her to discuss sex roles. In her seminal work, *Male and Female* (1949), she attempted to demonstrate the truth of Freudian sex theory with her anthropological observations. She concluded that, while there are exceptions, most cultures organize sex roles around the predisposing and particular limiting factors associated with the reproductive requirements placed on women by their physiology. She believed that while it is possible, and even desirable, for men to perform childcare functions and while there are some tribal settings in which the men do take responsibility for childcare, it is more convenient and practical for women to do the tasks of childcare and homemaking due to the physiological variables predisposing them to those tasks.[8] Hers was an attempt to prescribe for 20th-century western women behaviors that had been observed in nonwestern and nontechnological settings: that is, what is there is what ought to be everywhere.[9]

Erikson and Kohlberg

Erikson was trained in psychoanalysis, but came to believe that Freud's theories of psychosexual development did not pay sufficient attention to the social context in which ego development occurred. He de-emphasized the importance of the id and the superego and proceeded to create a model of human development that was psychosocial. His model introduced and validated philosophically a more interpersonal framework for psychological maturation. He emphasized the relational aspects of development by regarding the person's (especially, the child's) growth as occurring in a broad social milieu. His model proposed eight stages of maturation that the individual moves through more or less sequentially from birth to death: (a) Trust v. Mistrust, (b) Autonomy v. Shame and doubt, (c) initiative versus guilt, (d) industry versus inferiority, (e) Identity v. Identity diffusion, (f) Intimacy v. Isolation, (g) Generativity v. Self-absorption, and (h) Integrity v. Despair. In the first stage, the newborn is entirely dependent on the caregiver. Erikson believed that the environment from which separation must occur was the "other" (mother?). He did not view her as a mutual partner interconnected with the child in a process of growth (see Jordan et al., 1991)

Current critiques (see Chodorow, 1978; Gilligan, 1982; Josselson, 1992; Miller, 1976) suggest that Erikson was expressing male bias by defining maturity as the ability to perform independent, instrumental work, while assigning less importance to the need for interpersonal connection or intimacy. Erikson has been understood as claiming that identity formation precedes and determines the potential for intimacy. The critique suggests that Erikson overstated the need to develop independence and autonomy of function while understating the need for developing significant positive attachments to others in the environment.

Bem (1975) has challenged Erikson's (1964) description of maleness as focused on "outer space" and of femaleness as focused on "inner space." This differentiation was based on Erikson's observations of girls building low, encircling structures and boys building tall, jutting structures during pre-school play with blocks. He believed that these different foci led men to be more instrumental and agentic ("masculine") in their life activities, while they led women to be more conciliatory and healing ("feminine") in theirs.

Chodorow (1978) and Gilligan (1982) have suggested that a methodological flaw, the over-representation of men and boys in his samples, led Erikson to draw conclusions about what is "normal" and "healthy" for people from observations of what is "typical" of western European and North American men and boys. Erikson further compounded his error when he made generalizations about problems in women's development based on observation of males. He labeled as problematic women's tendency to give affiliative needs precedence. Thus, Erikson (and much of the women's movement of the 1970s) suggested that the typical goals of women to marry and have children were abnormal and unhealthy because women did not place equal or more value on independence and mastery than they did on maintaining their significant interpersonal relationships.

Kohlberg focused on superego development, that is, the development of moral reasoning and ethical decision-making, following the work on cognitive development done by Piaget (Kohlberg, 1958, 1969, 1973, 1976, 1981). This work has also been critiqued as methodologically flawed due to the underrepresentation of women and girls in the experimental samples, and due to its male bias in over-emphasizing the value of the individual's right to freedom of action (Baumrind, 1987; Gilligan, 1982).

Late Twentieth-Century Feminism

Simone de Beauvoir (1952) was a French existential philosopher who examined the roles of women in western European culture. Her conclusion was that women were regarded as the "second sex" due to western enlightenment values which placed a very high regard on rational thought and instrumental activity, especially as means useful in overcoming nature and nature's limitations on human achievement. Historically, women and the feminine have been assigned a close association with nature, suggesting that the conquest and control of nature included the conquest and control of woman, women, and the feminine. She believed that men were unable to recognize women as separate individuals having their own agency. She believed that men, who were in charge of naming, could only name woman "Other" because they were imprisoned by their own subjectivity, and thus women were necessarily the objectified ones. This tradition of thought continues in the contemporary epistemologies of French existentialist feminists such as Luce Irigaray.

In *The Feminine Mystique*, Friedan (1963) critiqued sociology, anthropology, and psychology for their psychoanalytically biased approach to sex roles. She became an advocate for the notion that women can and should be self-determining agents, in much the same ways that men have been. Her thought marked the beginning of the second wave of women's liberation that argued for the development of women's autonomy and independence economically, socially, and occupationally. She encouraged women to become self-defining and independent of men; she urged women to complete their suspended developmental tasks of establishing autonomy and identity. She and other feminists and psychotherapists challenged women to end their moratoria and their foreclosures on identity (i.e., occupation or career) formation. However, her encouragement rested on implicit acceptance of masculine definitions of success and masculine descriptions of masculine meanings of maturity as being the same as accomplished performance in one of the professions in a public environment.[10]

Sandra Bem and androgyny

In the middle and late 1970s, discussions of "androgyny" became common (Bem, 1974; Broverman et al., 1970, 1972; Maccoby & Jacklin, 1974; Money & Ehrhardt, 1972). In order to counter discrimination in the workplace and to allow well-educated women to pursue professional career goals outside the home for pay, it became a standard that there were no "real" sex differences, that all differences were the result of biased education and socialization or of simple prejudice, that if little boys and girls were treated in identical ways throughout their early development, sex differences would disappear. In an effort to demonstrate the reality and benefits of androgyny, Bem (1974) developed a Sex-Role Inventory. She and her colleagues at

Stanford first generated a list of over 400 sex-role attributes. From this list 20 positive "masculine" and 20 positive "feminine" attributes were identified and rated by college undergraduates as to whether or not and to what extent they described masculinity or femininity (see Table 3). Words which showed high agreement across subjects on masculinity and on femininity, respectively, were used in the androgyny scale. Twenty sex-role neutral and socially positive attributes were included to control for a social-desirability response bias. In the final step of constructing the inventory, other groups of college students were told to rate themselves as to how well these 60 attributes described them. With this instrument, Bem was able to discover feminine-identified, masculine-identified, undifferentiated, and androgynous types of individuals (see Table 1).

According to Bem's research findings, any individual may express high or low masculinity and high or low femininity. Those individuals who select many masculine and many feminine words to describe themselves were designated "androgynous" (see Table 1). This inventory is used widely in sex-role research, and findings often describe the mental health benefits of androgyny.

While the term "androgynous" was intended to refer to persons who function behaviorally and affectively in both masculine and feminine ways, for many people the word has conjured images of physical and emotional sexlessness, the bisexuality often seen in Rorschach Card III, or the dominance of maleness. "Androgyny" in fashion was prescribed for women by John Molloy (1977) in *Dress-for-Success*: The straight-lined, dark-colored business suit. This image was replaced by softer and more flowing, more curve-fitting suits and dresses in the 1980s, which have been followed by brilliant and eye-catching third-world fabrics and designs in the 1990s. It seems that many women are not satisfied with clothing that appears sexless or that is modeled on males' professional clothing.

Identity Development and Sex Difference

In her book, *The Reproduction of Mothering*, Chodorow (1978) attempted an analysis of Freud's assumptions about gender-identity formation and its relation to biology. Her basic conclusion was that men form their gender identity out of a reaction against and rejection of the mother and her dominance in the young male child's early life. She further suggested that women's task of identity formation may be somewhat less complicated than men's because women do not have to deal with the psychic threats created by the physical difference between the primary love-object (mother) and the child. The girl child never has had to repudiate the mother and the mother's body in the same way that a male child does in his attempts to establish himself as a person separate from the mother. Chodorow suggested that this sense of rejection and repudiation that the little boy must[11] experience leads to a breach in his relationships with women which is difficult to heal. She further suggested that because boys often take this step of identity formation in a setting where fathers are absent, boys have more difficulty in establishing positive definitions of maleness and masculinity. According to Chodorow's formulation, men develop their first sense of self as "not mother" and their sense of the mother-other as "not me"; these negations lead to a pervasive unconscious attitude of rejection, aggression or violence toward women and femininity.[12]

Chodorow suggested finally that the corrective in children's development that will heal the distortions that occur in traditional environments is for fathers to be more present, available and involved in the child-rearing task.[13] I believe that in order for father-presence to be healing and helpful, those fathers must also be aware of and working on healing their own distortions of femininity and masculinity. Fathers and mothers and other primary caregivers must examine and correct some profound, and largely unproven, negative assumptions about mothers and mothering (Bly, 1990; Johnson, 1990; Sebald, 1976; Swigart, 1991) that lead to a defensive rejection of "femininity" and selection of "masculinity" in male children and to a profound rejection and devaluation of "femininity" and exaltation of "masculinity" in female children. A further problem with dynamic formulations of identity formation is their overemphasis on the role of parents (primarily the mother) and a lack of awareness of sibling influences. These theories also underestimate the role of other family and community members, leading to bias in assuming the primacy of a nuclear family structure.

Sex and Gender Difference

Gilligan's work has been described in Chapter 1. Much of the critique of her research has focused on her claims that the data demonstrate differences between the sexes. Her critics have expressed fear that her work could be used to keep women out of leadership and the professions; they fear that acknowledgment of "difference" will reinforce discrimination against women (Gilligan, 1994). However, it is also true that her work could be used to keep men from developing healthier and more satisfying relationships; it could be used to discriminate against men in certain professions in which care-giving is deemed the vital trait.

In either case the difficulty is not with data. The difficulty is in drawing erroneous conclusions that Gilligan's (or any others') findings are in some way statements of universal and absolute truth about the essential nature of men and women. It is not clear that Gilligan is asserting that women connect and care because they are female, or that men separate and lack capacity to care because they are male. Rather, Gilligan has described social behavior that arises in a complex environment of biological, social, and psychological variables. One of the most important features of this environment, vis-à-vis gender, is its function in assigning value, positive and negative, to expression of some traits and to suppression of others. Men and women and girls and boys might do otherwise if they were trained and rewarded to do otherwise. This process of valuation is particularly important to the discussion of gender identity formation; that is, the way in which females and males become masculine and feminine is strongly shaped by what value is assigned to those traits and behaviors in individuals of each sex by the significant others in their social environment.[14]

Gilligan has continued her educational research on differences between men and women. In *Mapping the Moral Domain* (1988) and *Making Connections* (1990), she and her colleagues described research with males and females that trace the development of sex differences in learning and self-expression to latency stage and early adolescence. She made suggestions for accommodating educational methods and goals to the special needs of girls. Her primary concern is in enhancing young women's educational environment so that their learning will be optimal and so that they will complete high school and college. Her goal is to help girls and women become self-affirming so that they become educated and financially self-supporting.

In focusing on educational goals she sets aside larger and more holistic issues of personality formation. While she identifies difference as a fact which must be attended to in creating and implementing educational methods, she does not adequately address the valuing processes of the society that continue to emphasize career development and the public workplace as markers of achievement. For instance, why is it that as caregiving occupations which were male-dominated (such as teaching, clerical support, and counseling) become female-dominated they become less well-paid and men begin to leave the professions? Further, why is it that men who remain in these occupations move increasingly into "higher" management positions in which they exert authority over those who provide direct care and no longer deal directly with the ones cared for? What are the implicit rules of value of various gender attributes that influence these cultural shifts? How are gender and sex related to one another in such a case?

Belenky et al. (1986), in *Woman's Ways of Knowing*, have suggested that women use different epistemologies from men, based on different kinds of cognitive learning tasks and learning environments. Women develop "connected-knowing" strategies, that is, they know in relation with the thing or person known. The authors do not address how these differences are related to biological sex. Rather than focusing on how these differences come to be, they have continued an important work of describing differences as they currently exist. However, attempting some investigation of how difference comes to be is significant to assigning and reassigning value, and to reducing guilt and shame associated with particular behaviors and attitudes.

One of the early feminist psychologists to address the issue of sex difference was Jean Baker Miller (1976) in *Toward a New Psychology of Women*. She emphasized the particular and unique features of women's ways, and advocated a positive valuing of them. She also critiqued social conventions in the United States in the 1970s as overly valuing maleness and masculinity. Following and building on Miller's work, Jordan et al. (1991) have been researching and describing new models of human development that more accurately reflect girls' and women's experience. They have described the self-in-relation in order to describe more accurately the experience of women and the problems that women face. They articulate new perspectives on issues such as anger, success, empathy, mutuality, dependency, food, and power. They suggest that women's relationships to these issues is different from men's due to differential training and valuing. These authors observed that the treatment they were providing for women was not altogether effective. They wanted to know how to create more effective treatment, a search which led them to reconsider what constituted disturbance in the first place. Their work is significant in attempting to identify and disentangle value from fact; in encouraging careful analysis of what is and how it has come to be; in not labeling behavior and attitudes as pathological or abnormal if they are the valued and expected behaviors for a majority of the population, albeit the nondominant members. However, they, like Gilligan (1982), do not reflect on how, or even if, what they observe in women vis-à-vis men is biologically determined. They, like Gilligan and Belenky et al. (1986), imply without careful reflection and analysis, that somehow biological sex (i.e., "womanness" or "femaleness") is determinant of women's experience.

The Men's Movement has emerged as a social force as well. It began in the late 1960s as part of the Vietnam war protest. In the 1970s this movement took the form of encouraging men to become feminist and to become more in touch with and accepting of their "femininity" (Chesler, 1994; Farrell, 1975, 1988; Johnson, 1974, 1989a, 1991; Keen, 1991, Nelson, 1988). In the 1980s attention turned to the violence and hostility for which men were supposedly responsible (Dalbey, 1988; Kivel, 1992; Nelson, 1988). In the late 1980s and early 1990s some members of the men's movement expressed concern that men were no longer men but wimps (Bly, 1990), while others continued to emphasize the role that maleness and masculinity have in the perpetration of violence (Miedzian, 1991).

Two books on sex differences which have enjoyed wide popularity are *Men Are from Mars; Women Are from Venus* (Gray, 1992)[15] and *Brainsex* (Moir & Jessel, 1991). The difficulty with these two works is that they overstate the findings and interpretations of sex differences and their behavioral consequences. Their work reinforce common misunderstandings of maleness as aggressive, instrumental, and active, and of femaleness as submissive, emotive, and passive. Gray presents anecdotal information about male and female behavior, using sex and gender caricatures to tease and chastise couples for not accommodating their "natural" sex differences. His jocular and devaluing attitude is itself a caricature of masculinity and its cultural function of directing and coercing change. Moir and Jessel overestimate the dominance of biology, and imply or state overly simplistic relationships between biology and social learning. They suggest that most, if not all, sex differences can be explained by the influence of sex hormones during gestation and puberty, especially by the effects of high levels of testosterone on the development of the male brain and on consequent male aggressiveness. While there is increasing evidence that there are hormonal differences that do affect a variety of human traits, the differences and their effects are not so straightforward as these authors imply (Brod, 1987; Jacklin, 1989; Maccoby, 1990; Pleck, 1981; Riger, 1992).

Relatedness and Psychoanalytic Thought

Several recent psychoanalytic thinkers have added features of interpersonal connection to their theories, but this addition has not translated into theories that are more sympathetic to "women's' ways." I have already considered the contributions of Erikson in describing the importance of the social milieu. Sullivan (1953) also emphasized the social nature of human experience. He explicated a model of growth and change that emphasized the shaping force of interpersonal encounters. He described a sense of self that included repudiated parts of the personality, the sense of the "not me," but he did not apply these notions to gender identity formation. It is likely that he, as did his contemporaries, assumed that his theories applied equally to men and women. In general his theories seem less pathologizing than many.

Other clinical theorists, such as Bowlby (1969), Klein (1957), Mahler (1975), and Winnicott (1963), have created elaborate theories about the importance of the mother-infant relationship to the healthy growth of the infant or child. However, the relatedness they describe is fusion of an inchoate bundle of drives (the infant) to an "object" (the mother) that is used by the infant for the satisfaction of internal physiological drives (Jordan et al., 1991). Thus, development consists in the infant's increasing awareness that the caregiver is a separate person who is free to refuse the infant's demands, which precipitates a crisis for the child that is resolved by the development of independent self-care.

In this case the most salient features of the theorists' explication of gender are in their depictions of the mother as an unending supply of nurture. The mother becomes not "not man" with no penis, nor "woman" with receiving vaginaand uterus. Rather, she becomes "woman" with breast (especially in the work of Klein). Again, woman is defined as a biological part; her value resides in the fullness of her breast. Woman is now defined by her fitness for the child. Winnicott (1971) goes so far as to state that the mother is uniquely prepared by her biology to meet the emotional needs of her child with unselfishness and without depletion, a fantastic conclusion which any mother (especially one who has suffered a biologically induced postpartum depression) knows is not so. As in other cases in which woman's nature is deduced from her biology, she does not have value and being in and of, or for, herself. These theorists, unlike Chodorow, suggest that the father can be only secondarily involved with the infant's development. The father's role during infancy is to care for the mother[16] and his role after the child begins its separation is to direct the child away from the mother and to protect the child from reengulfment by the mother (Mahler, 1975; Gooch & Noble, 1989).[17]

Stern (1985) has been studying infant behavior and describing a model of infant development that views the infant as an independent and interdependent agent in the environment from birth onwards. His research is challenging analytic conceptions of the mother because it is challenging analytic conceptions of the child. However, it is yet to be seen if he will reformulate the infant-mother relationship in such a way as to free the mother's self from the tyranny of the infant's need. This freedom could have an immense impact on future descriptions of woman and man, masculine and feminine.

Conclusion

For hundreds of years, masculinity and femininity have been closely linked with biological sex, male and female, respectively. In the course of human history femaleness has been considered to be inferior to maleness, especially due to its close association in philosophical and theological discourse with nature, matter, dirt, and carnality (lust and concupiscence). In the late 19th century and the early 20th century, attempts were made to explain observed psychological, emotional and ethical differences between men and women by interpreting observations of biological functioning. However, those observations and interpretations were contaminated by widely held, but largely unsubstantiated, assumptions about the value of maleness and femaleness which had been inherited from earlier eras. In the middle of the 20th century social roles were prescribed for women and men as if biology were absolutely determinant. Beginning in the 1960s, researchers and philosophers began to challenge assumptions that biology unilaterally determined social behavior. The disciplines of education and psychology prescribed corrections so that women could develop autonomy and independence, while they encouraged men to develop the relational and emotional aspects of their personalities. "Androgyny," the ability of women and men to function in both "masculine" and "feminine" modes, became more popular. However, women seem to have adopted more "masculinity" than men have "femininity" (Brod, 1987; Pleck, 1981). Further, some fear that "androgyny" means that people will become either "asexual" or "masculine" only (Wolf, 1992). More recently, researchers and commentators have suggest that important differences do exist in the social patterns of women and men. However, the causes of these differences is not well-established. Some commentators fear a backlash attempt to reestablish traditional sex-roles—and, with them, the subordination of women—as normative: masculinity for men and femininity for women (Faludi, 1991).

With this review of the history of thought regarding sex and gender completed, it is now possible to turn to consideration of femininity and the social mechanisms which induce feelings of shame in individuals who attempt to express their femininity. Due to recurrent themes in theology, philosophy, and the social sciences that devalue and denigrate the feminine, men and women continue to reject parts of their personalities and their behavioral repertoires that could otherwise inform and transform social discourse and social behavior; they silence the feminine voice.

Chapter 4.
Shame and Femininity

"And they were both naked, the man and [woman], and were not ashamed."
                                                        Genesis 2:25 (KJV)

In this study we have been investigating the relationship between women's sense of self, voicelessness, and femininity. Some recent findings suggest that women's experience differs from men's in significant ways (Belenky et al., 1986; Chodorow, 1978; Gilligan, 1982; Gilligan et al., 1988; Gilligan et al., 1990; Jordan et al., 1991). The differences may be summarized as follows: Women experience the self as connected to others, while men experience the self as separated from others. Researchers have suggested that the woman's way, connection and care, is often silenced in conventional educational and work settings. Other psychologists, including Bem (1974) and E. Jung (1972), have described femininity in terms similar to connection and care and have suggested that the feminine may exist in both men and women; Jung, Adler, Ferenczi, and Rank believed that the feminine is typically forced out of awareness, especially by men, as the personality develops in conventional western cultural contexts. Other, contemporary, theorists also believe that femininity is repudiated by men in the formation of male identity (Bly, 1990; Chesler, 1978; Chodorow, 1978; Dinnerstein, 1976; Hillman, 1985; Johnson, 1974; E. Jung, 1972; Miller, 1976).

Shame and Gender

A survey of the history of sex and gender has highlighted many ways in which women have been exposed to shaming environments in western culture. In the Dark Ages and the Middle Ages women were accused of seducing men into sexual sin because women had voracious sexual appetites and were less moral than men. In the 19th century women were given responsibility for civilizing men because women had no "animalistic" sex drive. In both eras women were thought to be intellectually inferior and were limited in their access to political self-determination, even though their moral characters were portrayed in extremely divergent ways. Women's roles and experiences have been limited by men, because of his relationship to his and her sexuality (de Beauvoir, 1952; Brown, 1988; Ranke-Heinemann, 1990).

Women and Femininity

In the late 1800s in Europe fear and awe of women's sexuality shifted in its focus to women's dependency and vulnerability, so that Adler (1910/1956) could state that the masculine protest of the growing child was against the weakness, cowardice, and submissiveness of the feminine. Following the arguments of Sampson (1993) and Cushman (1990), I suggest that the development of a cultural identity for woman as dependent and vulnerable would support the industrialization of production and the labor force. Later in the middle of the 20th century, that same cultural portrayal of woman would create a consumer for a consumption economy. The stereotype of the vulnerable, dependent woman prevailed in American culture well into the 20th century.

Roberta Bondi (1995), in her recent memoir, describes her understanding of her womanhood and femininity as being shaped by her father's views of men and women.: Men were intelligent, determined, able to hold their own in any argument; women, on the other hand, were compliant, demure, silent. Bondi found that she could not be for her father what a woman was supposed to be, so she felt unloved and unlovely. Nor could she be what she was: intelligent, strong, determined--like a man--for fear of her father's contempt of masculine females. Trapped in her father's stereotypes, she could be other than she knew herself to be and be valued; or she could be herself and be despised. Her solution was to hide herself from her father and feel ashamed. She expresses what many women recognize: Shame at being "woman."

A female client who grew up in the fifties said, as she struggled to complete her graduate studies:

> To do the task a woman's way in a man's world. That's what I want ... but I experience great resistance in myself, to both the woman's way *and* the man's way. ... which am I? ... it's easier, less painful, to go hide.

These women know something of feeling ashamed of being a woman and of wanting to be free to be like a man, in the capacity to assert and to do. Women are increasingly permitted satisfaction of their masculine strivings. Although it may be difficult for a woman to work in an all male environment, it is becoming increasingly possible. Although there is certainly a glass ceiling in American business (Faludi, 1991), a few women are leading corporations. In another arena, women cannot cross-dress. It is impossible: Women may wear any kind of "mens-wear". However, the sight of a male in feminine dress would still be considered highly comic or downright perverse in most common social settings today. Women's ways, the feminine, may be muted because women choose not to speak and men choose not to hear. The average American man is socially limited in his expression of femininity. Femininity in males may seem nonexistent, except in prurient forms, because there is so much shame associated with men's expression of their femininity.

Men and Femininity

According to Kaplan (1991), the sexual perversions are found almost exclusively among males and the main goal of the perverse strategy is to satisfy the man's "feminine strivings" while hiding them from himself and the world. Further, she states that the goal of the behaviors is not to "make love, but to make hate" (p. 40). She suggests that the male perversions are attempts to gain control over dark, scary, dangerous females.[1] While most men do not practice the perversions, there is evidence that men are afraid of femininity and that the development of their sense of self is in reaction against the feminine (Adler, 1910; Bly, 1990, Chodorow, 1978; Freud, 1905, Levinson, 1978). According to Adler (1910/1956) each person is some combination of strong and willful, of weak and obedient, but for some reason many men have come to understand their own feelings of compliance and tenderness as deplorable, as shameful, and as feminine. In an article on how men are trained to violence in American professional sports, Lipsyte (1994) states that American boys are trained to act not "like girls." He tells of a football coach who chastises his team for poor performance by placing sanitary napkins in the lockers. Coaches discourage players from contact with women that will "soften" players, weaken their performance, and decrease the coach's control. This coach's behavior is in fact sexual harassment. Why is it so humiliating for a man to be treated like a women?

Chodorow (1978) has been credited with reformulating the concept of the Oedipal conflict in a way that more adequately incorporates the girl's experience in describing her emerging sense of self. She redefined the boy's experience such that he develops an identity of negation vis-à-vis the mother-other.[2] Chodorow supports the analytic thesis that the boy separates from the mother in order to avoid reengulfment, to consolidate his independence, and to establish his identity in relationship with the father. This model has appeal because it gives the female a face of her own, but I question the validity of an emphasis on the mother as such an overpowering determinant of the son's and daughter's identities. Even without a father in the home, there are other male, and female, figures in the child's life such as siblings (who have great influence) and neighbors. What does appear to be accurate in Chodorow's description is the cultural emphasis on encouraging the boy toward early autonomy, and away from the expression of femininity.

According to Ullian (1981), typically masculine traits are established in the young boy's behavioral repertoire between the ages of 4 and 7. If he feels somehow that he does not meet the standard for masculinity, he will still attempt to conform to the social ideals for adult male strength, size, and prowess, even to the point of exaggeration. Stevens and Gardner (1994)[3] find that parents reinforce boys in their adoption of exaggerated masculinity and their rejection of feminine behavior. They state that boys are ill-served by attempts to make them more masculine. They cite research that demonstrates that "the males of our species, not the females, are the 'weaker' sex" (p. 27). They believe that boys who are pressed to early autonomy are especially likely to suffer later in life from problems stemming from "a confused sense of identity and greater separation anxiety" (p. 26). These authors go on to state that men are socialized to deny their own dependency and desires for closeness, and simultaneously are taught to dominate women intimates. This socialization begins at an extremely early age, and forces boys to behave in ways for which they are constitutionally unfit. "In direct contradiction to the constitutional differences between the sexes . . . social forces—as reflected, for example, in traditional child-rearing practices—have defined autonomy as 'masculine'" (p. 2). Traditional sex roles ignore or distort enduring constitutional and maturational differences between men and women, including men's need for ongoing connection with significant others. Stevens and Gardner cite the work of Angyal (1941)[4] and Spieler (1986) in support of their claim that American male children are forced into premature autonomy and out of homonomy (Angyal's term for the tendency to attach, to seek comfort and emotional connection). According to Sears, Maccoby and Levin (1957), the child's denial of dependency needs leads to increased efforts to satisfy dependency needs. Thus, boys are seen engaged in behavior that creates a negative feedback loop, and constant deprivation. Stevens and Gardner (1994) state that this early deprivation establishes patterns of beliefs and behavior that continue into adulthood. Adult males expect to be deprived. For example, an upper middle-class white male was discussing the competitive behavior of his employees. He was troubled that they could not cooperate and share resources even though he had portrayed the resources as scarce. Perhaps, he had been socially conditioned in childhood by becoming desensitized to unsatisfied dependency and attachment needs. Stevens and Gardner also suggest that men expect women to be the ones who deprive men.

Steven and Gardner (1994) also report that males are more likely to suffer from genetic and physiological abnormalities that put them at risk during infancy and childhood for the development of illness and behavioral dysfunction. Boys' physiological and cognitive development lags behind girls'. In adulthood, men are more prone to stress-related illnesses, have higher rates of depression and successful suicide, and higher incidence of fatal illnesses than women. Stevens and Gardner conclude that there is

a subtle pathogenic element in the typical social learning experiences of males: society exacts greater demands for autonomy, unrelatedness, individual strength, and resourcefulness as goals of males than females, despite the fact that males are less biologically equipped to meet these demands. (p. 45)[5]

Perhaps Adler (1910/1956) spoke a greater truth than he knew about male children, when he described the generic child's "masculine protest" in the face of sickness and deficiency. The litany of male deficiencies creates a far different picture of men and masculinity than has been portrayed by cultural sex-role stereotypes of men as dominant, individualistic, strong, and sexually virile. Perhaps, there is reason for men and boys to feel self-consciousness, and, yes, even shame. To know oneself as weak and needy in the face of a cultural ideal of supreme strength and invincibility is likely to create a proneness to shame.

How is the cultural ideal transmitted to boys, and how does it become internalized as a specific ego ideal? How does femininity come to be associated with the failure of masculinity and then become silenced? Young males who live in a relationally deprived environment may finally give up their attempts to gain satisfaction from that socioemotional environment. Like the rat who eventually stops pushing the lever when no food pellets appear or like the dog who finally settles into depressed toleration of electric shocks when he cannot make them stop, perhaps, male children give up trying to engage their mothers after the mothers remain nonresponsive. Mothers are not the only adults involved in raising their sons. Many and various adults, including fathers, communicate to boys that they ought to be without need and that neediness will neither be tolerated nor satisfied. Thus, boys may receive high levels of negative attention (positive reinforcement) for their neediness but no satisfaction of the needs. To be dependent on unfulfilling and humiliating "others" is shaming.

The image of the needy and deficient, but ignored, male raises an interesting possibility: In a recent review of the literature on sex differences, Maccoby (1990) found that little boys were nonresponsive to little girls' verbal prohibitions when they were in partnered play situations together. Maccoby suggested boys learned from observing their parents' interchanges that males don't listen to females; however, she states that the behavior of ignoring is present earlier than would be possible for reliable recognition of sex difference to occur. She also suggested that the girl reminds the boy of mother; this alternative explanation would be in keeping with the presentation of Stevens and Gardner that little boys learned from their mothers and other caregivers that females are not reliably present, then boys adopt an in-kind response pattern to all females. However, fathers also do not respond to their sons' needs with satisfaction of need (Stevens & Gardner, 1994). Fathers then are also not reliably present. Maccoby (1990) also highlights the finding that males in same-sex and cross-sex groups interact in directive and dominant modes while girls interact in mutual and cooperative modes. Boys in boys' groups were also less likely to listen to adults than to each other, suggesting that boys become increasingly separated from the larger societal unit while bonding to one another, presenting a picture of boys raising themselves. Add to this male separatism, the autonomous and aggressive role models to which boys have easiest access: television, video game, and comic book superheroes. Boys are powerfully influenced to develop disaffiliated dominance. Stevens and Gardner (1994) suggest that males who have not adequately attached in infancy, who have not received adequate nurturance and satisfaction of dependency in early childhood, grow into disadvantaged boys and men who have fewer emotional resources and narrower behavioral repertoires for obtaining gratification of their needs then adequately attached and nurtured children. This situation leads to the formation of the "Umbilicus Complex," a state in which boys and men are extremely susceptible to the disorganizing influence of loss due to the presence of separation anxiety or dread of abandonment that is rooted in the particular forms of emotional and physical deprivations experienced during infancy and early childhood. Boys and men with such experience and beliefs must have difficulty with expression of masculinity as well.

Masculinity and Shame

It would be easy to think of all deprivation as originating with the mother since she is usually the child's primary source of care, but the father must also bear some responsibility. If boys and men are ashamed of their femininity, their sense of lack, then they recognize at times that they had to become that way. The analytic framework suggests that the threat is that the boy will be "unmanned" by the father. If we allow the analytic metaphor, the boy loses his "manhood" at the father's hand to become the despised feminine. Castration, albeit emotional, will contribute to the boy's, and so the man's, shame. Monick (1991) gives the following example of a father's castrating rage:

> An analysand told me that at the age of six or seven, his father took him for a winter hike in the mountains. There was snow on the ground. The boy was walking ahead of his father along the trail. The father stopped to urinate, then called for the son to return to where he was. When the son did so, the father pointed to the words he had spelled in the snow with his urine: George is a baby. (p. 80)

According to Monick, that father had castrated his son. Aggressively hostile and belittling action drew instant recognition from the son, and the father's ridicule has been the son's burden ever since. In another case, I was walking in the desert with a former Marine and his 4 year old son. The son fell, tumbling down the hillside for several feet. When he rose his knees and hands were bloody, he was covered in dirt, and his shirt was torn. He was holding back tears, but was sniffing, which caused dirt to get in his nose, which then caused him to sneeze. As he sniffed and sneezed, his father became more agitated and yelled, "Stupid, sonofabitch, stop snorting like a bitch in heat! Suck it up! Be a goddamn man!" According to Monick's frame, the father castrated his son that day. The father wounded the son's masculinity; it is likely that the father gave as he had been given. These encounters with the unmanned, castrating father unman the son, and the result must be the severest form of shame. In these examples there is an explicit biological reductionism that is common to analytic thought. Even without the metaphors of phallic identification, feminine disidentification, and castration, the humiliation experienced by these boys and inflicted by their fathers would be extremely hurtful and detrimental to their developing sense of themselves.

According to Stevens and Gardner (1994), divorced men who suffer dread of abandonment are full of rage (see Lansky, 1987, 1992; Myers, 1989; Wallerstein & Blakaslee, 1990; Weiss, 1975). Revenge and retaliation will dominate their fantasies, and they may choose to act on them. If violence is expressed in intimate relationships, it may serve the adaptive, yet abnormal function, of maintaining the relationship. Stevens and Gardner have called a man in this kind of emotional, relational situation a "pasha-babe," one who at once yearns to have his needs met by a powerful other and seeks a relationship with women by dominating, controlling, and coercing the source of his need fulfillment.

According to the findings of sociobiology and evolutionary biology, humans are extremely aggressive when compared to other animals, and the male human is especially aggressive and violent (Ardrey, 1966; Fromm, 1973; Jacklin, 1989; Lorenz, 1963; Moir & Jessel, 1991; Nathanson, 1992; Stevens & Gardner, 1994). However, expression of aggression is probably due to some interaction between learning and physiological predisposing factors, especially circulating testosterone. Stevens and Gardner (1994) suggest two root causes of violence against women, "sexual jealousy and acting out matricidal fantasies" (p. 130) which may take forms that range from mass murder to rape to torture to domestic violence. Forms of sexual mutilation occur in many cultures. Decreasing family involvement in the supervision of dating and increasing influence of peers on men's self-esteem may be factors contributing to increased violence in these relationships. According to Stevens and Gardner,

> hatred of women has become more naked and virulent. ... The motivation for the denigration of women has as its source primitive rage [and as a way to] avenge early rejection by the mother ... [to] rebel against authority, [to redress envy of women, and to express] devaluation of the primary object of dependency. ... [it is] the defensive denial by men of their own powerlessness. (p. 139)

The interpersonal dynamics described by Stevens and Gardner are replete with possibilities for evocation of shame: Denial, passivity, envy, rage, lack of self love, and threat to bodily integrity make pasha-babes highly vulnerable to shame.

Historically, women have been severely inhibited in their expression of masculinity. When Jung first used the term "animus-identified" to connote a woman expressing instrumental and independent behavior, he meant that she was misbehaving and described the behaviors in value-laden, pejorative terms; throughout the early analytic literature for a woman to be male-identified, animus-identified, or masculinized was to be sick or neurotic or maladjusted, to be someone who had to be fixed. There is evidence that this kind of thinking about achieving women still exists in contemporary American culture. For instance, a few years ago, the former CEO of a large stock brokerage confided to me that all the top women executives that he knew in his profession were "lonely, bitter, unhappy women" who "couldn't have a relationship if they tried" and "they wouldn't even try" because they were too "damaged" in the first place to even know that they should have relationships. Men, on the other hand, are severely inhibited in their expression of their femininity. At one time, repudiation of feminine behavior may have been protective, saving the individual and his clan from death. However, in the late 20th century perceptions of the need for autonomous mastery and rejection of cooperative satisfaction of mental needs are endangering the human race (Bellah et al., 1985; Cushman, 1990; Sampson, 1978, 1993). Both women and men must have access to both masculinity and femininity without being shamed. Shame, its mechanisms, and its role in limiting expressions of genderality will now be explored.

Shame

In the preceding sections, I provided support for the thesis that the feminine is devalued and denigrated and that women, who have typically expressed femininity for all members of the culture, have been treated in ways that induce shame in relation to their femininity. And, it was shown that men also experience intense feelings of shame in relation to their femininity and attempt to avoid shame by (a) suppressing and repressing their own feminine strivings, (b) punishing women for men's dependent feelings, and (c) projecting femininity onto and into women.

People lose their voices and go into hiding when they are ashamed (Buber, 1947; Dunfee, 1982; Lewis, 1971). The experience of shame may be as mild as the chagrin one feels when she trips over her own feet, or as potent as the humiliation and annihilation one feels when he is told hostilely and repeatedly that he should never have been born. According to Nathanson (1987), the pathognomic expression of shame is covering the face. The feeling of shame is often described as wishing one could fall in a hole and disappear (Lewis, 1971).

The word *shame* is derived from a Middle English root which means "to hide [or] to cover," from the German word *skem* which means "hide or skin," and from a Latin root which means "shirt." It is defined as:

1: a painful emotion arising from the consciousness of something dishonoring, ridiculous, or indecorous in one's conduct or circumstances (or in others whose honor or disgrace one regard's as one's own) or of being in a situation that offends one's modesty or decency 2: fear of offense against propriety and decency—operating as a restraint on behavior. (*Merriam-Webster's Collegiate Dictionary*, 1993, p. 1126)

Guilt comes from a Middle English root which means "delinquency"; it is defined as "the fact of having committed a breach of conduct, especially violating law and involving penalty; broadly: guilty conduct; the state of one who has committed an offense, especially, consciously" (*Merriam-Webster's Collegiate Dictionary*, 1993, p. 517). It is obvious from the definitions that shame and guilt are related and that they differ. Most researchers currently believe that the two emotions are separate entities phenomenologically (Lewis, 1971; Nathanson, 1987; Wurmser, 1987). According to Nathanson (1987),

shame, like guilt, is an unpleasant emotion experienced as if it were directed by one agency of the self against another. Whereas guilt refers to punishment for wrongdoing, for violation of some sort of rule or internal law, shame implies that some quality of the self has been brought into question. (p. 4)

Lewis (1971) found that neurosis and the failure of superego functioning are related to the emotional experiences of shame and guilt. For many years, shame was subsumed under the rubric of guilt in most psychological literature. During the same period, the superego was thought of primarily in terms of its prohibiting and punishing function through the evolution of the "sense of guilt" (p. 21). However, the superego has a second component, the internalized imago of the ideal person, whom one wants to be like and to act like, which is called the "ego ideal." Failures of control are punished by external, and later internalized, authority figures and activate the sense of guilt, while failures to live up to the ego ideal are met with feared or real loss of love, which is internalized as loss of self-love and activates shame. According to Lewis (1971),

[i]n shame, the internalized admired imago functions more visibly [than in guilt] as the referent "in whose eyes" shame is experienced. ... the [ashamed] person does not experience the full affect of shame but rather has thoughts about what the "other" is thinking about the self. These "watching" thoughts may include the awareness that the person is thinking about what the other person is thinking about him. ... the self is both participant and watcher in its own fantasy. (pp. 23–24)[6]

While guilt has the purpose of regulating the drives in general, shame seems to have a special relationship to sexual activity and its inhibition (Lewis, 1971, 1981; Nathanson, 1987, 1992; Wurmser, 1987). In a broader sense shame is associated with regulation of intimacy and interest (Nathanson, 1987). Lewis (1971) states that shame serves the painful purpose of reminding the individual that the [inner] other who is the object of our longing is a "fantasy other . . . [and] that the other rejects the self" (p. 25). As such, shame can function positively to motivate the self to reclaim itself from the fantasy encounter, through achievement of some goal for and by the self.

Lewis (1971) maintains that psychological states may be categorized by (a) the presence or absence of affect; (b) the source of the affect, "self" of "other"; and (c) the direction of the affect, toward the self or the other. Then, she examines the definition of shame according to these categories in order to elaborate a description of shame as a psychological state. She concludes that shame is "a painful or negative emotion" (p. 64), while guilt may be more "objective." That the "other" is involved as a source of shame is a given since there can be no sense of dishonor or disgrace without some interpersonal referent. She also indicates that

shame may be experienced for someone else, as if the "other's" honor were one's own. In this meaning of the term, there is a feeling of personal responsibility, and yet the self is by implication helpless to avoid the shame of the "other" who is so close. (p. 64)

Shame may be directed toward the self or the other. However, the source and direction of shame is not simply the "other"; rather the shame comes from having given offense or having been immodest with respect to "the proper relationship between the self and the 'other.' . . . the object of the negative affect is unclear . . . it is their relationship which is at fault. Negative affect is directed against the situation" (p. 65). From these comments it appears that both the self and the other are involved in the experience of shame, even when the "other" is not physically present in the shame-evoking situation.

Shame can also be understood as a motive for avoiding behaviors that breach social contracts. According to Lewis (1971), shame is other-directed or other-determined in such cases. Because of its reference to the other, action based on shame has been considered by many theorists (Kohlberg, 1969, 1976) to express a "lower" form of morality than "guilt." The presence of shame has been viewed as indicating a less autonomous and less independent attitude, a view that, until quite recently, has been accepted unquestioned as defining human maturity. If the shame motivation leads one to act in a socially conforming way in order to avoid sanction rather than out of care for the other and its concomitant self-regard, perhaps, this designation of "lower" holds. However, as a safeguard and regulator of one's ability to abide by a mutually agreed upon social contract (Kohlberg, 1969, 1976), shame may function at a very advanced stage of moral decision-making.

Shame and Interpersonal Relatedness

Lewis (1971, 1981) states that shame is inherently interpersonal and that it serves to regulate social connection. According to Nathanson (1987), researchers observe a prototypical shame reaction in infants as early as two or three months of age. He believes that although it has no "meaning" at this early age, this "proto-shame" (p. 23) experience is the foundation upon which the emotion shame grows into being. In this early form, it signals the infant's recognition of the other as "other," where the "other" may be a person or a thing which interests the child. One of the infant's most charged "other" encounters is with his or her primary caregivers; thus, Nathanson concludes that typical stranger anxiety observed in 5- to 8-month old infants is really an early shame experience; this view is supported, he believes, by the presence of characteristic face-covering or face-hiding behavior. Following Tomkins (1987), Nathanson (1987) suggests that shame is one of nine affect mechanisms found in humans from birth onward that serve to communicate intense experience; shame affect is used to turn off intensely pleasurable experience that would otherwise continue to increase and finally overwhelm the infant. Over time and repeated experiences the shame affect is elaborated with meanings until the emotion shame emerges.

In older individuals for whom shame is a well-developed emotion-meaning system, shame reactions have several distinctive features (Lewis, 1971). Shame is evoked in situations that are characterized by the presence of aggression, defeat, disappointment, or failure, and especially as these are experienced in love and sex, even when there is no moral transgression. Shame is stimulated by what seems an involuntary event that brings into awareness a deficiency in the self, often in relation to some highly significant other. Shame is characterized by an affective component that (a) is experienced variously as states of mild sheepishness to states of intense humiliation; (b) is often expressed nonverbally through looking and gesturing; and (c) "is likely to involve autonomic reactions and awareness of the body" (p. 85), such as blushing. Shame is often accompanied by a hostility that is "diffuse and nonspecific, except that it is evoked by indications that the 'other' does not value the self" (p. 87). According to Lewis shame is dealt with by the individual in characteristic ways: One common defense mechanism is denial, which is a form of withdrawal and avoidance; another defense is the repression of ideas, or loss of cognitive contents; and a common behavioral defense is reaction formation, with personal achievement restoring positive self-love through narcissistic affirmation. If shame cannot be adequately discharged, the formation of symptoms of depression is often the result.

One particularly important aspect of phenomenal shame is its underlying self-other dynamic. Lewis (1971) describes evoked shame as a state in which the "other" is internally personified and is actively relating to the self. The self is perceived as disabled and little, with the result that the self becomes the object of scorn or contempt of the big "other"; the self is "helpless," "passive," and "paralyzed" in the face of the ridicule of the powerful "other." While the "other" appears to be mature, intact, and self-controlled, the self is experienced through "noxious body stimuli" such as "tears, rage, and blushing" that leave the self feeling childish, overwhelmed, and out of control. Finally, while the "other" is able to maintain cognitive and behavioral awareness, the self experiences distortions in perceptions and apperceptions of the self and the "other," as well as increased permeability in its self-other boundary such that the self is left prone to humiliation, especially because both the self and the "other" are focused on the self and its failure.

The opposite of shame is pride. According to Nathanson (1992), healthy pride is an affect or emotion that is part of the enjoyment-joy family, and is experienced as "competence pleasure." Pride is a combination of recognizing oneself and one's efficacy in an atmosphere of positive affect, enjoyment-joy. Further, pride prompts one to affiliate with others, to reach out in order to share mastery and its enjoyment. Enjoyment-joy is one of two positive affects, the other being interest-excitement. Nathanson states that

> . . . whatever causes an optimal increase in intensity and rate of activity of anything going on in the brain will trigger the affect interest. . . . The affect that Tomkins calls shame-humiliation is utterly and completely involved with the positive affects of interest-excitement and enjoyment-joy. Shame feels so miserable because it interrupts what feels best in life. (p. 73)

Shame is the response that the human organism has to protect itself from the difficulty of encountering impediments to interest, joy, and pride. When, in the throes of excitement or joy, one experiences an environmental threat to continuing those good feelings and to one's being itself, the brain-body responds with its own mechanism to turn off or to mute the good feelings; that mechanism is shame.

Shame, sex, and pride

According to Nathanson (1992), in the course of human development, pride and shame come to have a special relationship to the experiences of love, the "generative system" (p. 256f), and sexuality. Love is the desire for relatedness and nurturance; the generative system is the biogenetic sexual system; sexuality is the complex of biology and learned behavior that begins with arousal and ends with the relaxation after orgasm. Nathanson asserts the power of sexuality to captivate and to produce pleasure, and the definitive role of sexual dimorphism in the shaping of the sense of one's sexual self. He states that gender identity is comprised of an awareness of one's actual biological sex and an awareness of the meanings that the culture assigns to one's sex.

Nathanson (1992), following the work of Tabin (1985), suggests that infants experience physical sexual arousal from birth and begin learning about their sexual bodies at that time. As they learn about gender expectations, as they have encounters with sexed human beings, and as they gain experience with the powerful feelings of arousal, they gain a collection of visceral, cognitive, and affect data that create the complex relationship between sex, pride, and shame. Nathanson believes that parents respond negatively to their young children's sexual arousal in ways that belittle and humiliate the child for their sexual self-exploration. In this way, sexual arousal and its pleasure become closely associated with shame very early in life. He believes that functions related to the sex drive develop in four waves of increased awareness and capacity for satisfaction: In the neonatal period, in toddlerhood, in early childhood (during the Oedipal phase), and in adolescence. Physiological arousal comes into awareness as a desire to touch and to be touched.

Nathanson (1992) states that males experience sexual arousal as a highly visible and external event that anyone can see and over which they have little control; as a result, boys and men are extremely self-conscious, open to humiliation, and prone to shame. In contrast to males, females experience sexuality in a highly interiorized way. Even though the girl or woman may be experiencing intense arousal, that arousal will not be visible to casual bystanders, as a male's might be. Yet, the female also has experiences of arousal and sexual behavior that lead to shame-proneness. Because of the receptive function of the female genitals, women contain a variety of fluids that leak and smell, "thus, the woman is subject to self-dissmell and self-disgust merely because she is female. These affects, of course, keep company with shame" (p. 296).

Nathanson's (1992) descriptions of sexuality and sexual dimorphism stand in contrast to other data that minimize differences between men and women.[7] How powerful is embodiment? How critical is the functioning of the "generative system" to relations between the sexes? While sexual arousal certainly is intensely exciting and pleasurable, is it as centrally organizing as Nathanson's descriptions suggest? Nathanson:

> Sexual arousal exposes us to scrutiny of another person at a moment when we are ready to let ourselves be taken by forces that overwhelm us. . . . if intimacy is difficult, then it is that much more difficult for people to be both intimate and sexual. . . . Anything with so much power is likely to get out of control. . . . To know sex is to know shame. (pp. 300–301)

At the biological level, Nathanson's claim overstates the power of sexual experience. However, given the highly pleasurable nature of sexual behavior as well as the intense interpersonal interest and excitement that it generates, it is not surprising that the genitals may become focal metaphors or symbols for other less tangible but equally exciting and pleasurable experiences. Young children's arousal occurs in a variety of settings, some not interpersonal. Associating the excitement and interest of physical arousal to genital sexual expression is ocially directed, as is the pathological shame that often comes to be associated with the expression of sexuality. It is common for individuals to experience physiological signals like those of sexual arousal during intense periods of creative effort (Nathanson, 1992). A further difficulty with this description of sexual self-awareness is in its portrayal of cross-sexual encounters with opposite-sexed parents as normative. Little boys and girls experience arousal in the presence of various people of both sexes. Tabin's (1985) and Nathanson's (1992) accounts do not adequately explain these phenomena. One problem with focusing exclusively on genital experiences of arousal is that they become the only locus of understanding interest and excitement; the genitals as metaphor are interpreted literally.

This intense desire that the child feels for another person whom she/he may not have may lead the child to deny the longing or to reject the person or to envy and spoil the person in some way.

Sex, gender, and envy

Envy is human hate, an attack on life (Berke, 1987; Klein, 1957; Ulanov & Ulanov, 1983). Envy celebrates the occurrence of evil events in the life of another. Envy is the response one makes to another's good fortune when one is sure that good fortune will never be one's own because the good fortune is associated with the other's being. When one sees in the other the ideal, and despairs of ever being the ideal, then one feels shame. When one cannot redeem oneself in order to ward off the shame, one may fall into envy, the attitude that declares, "If I can't have it no one else will!" This attitude leads to attempts to spoil the goodness that is the other (Klein, 1957).

The concept of spoiling the envied person or the envied attributes of the person is especially relevant to the discussion of sexuality and genderality. The devaluation of femininity and female sexuality is a spoiling reaction to the envied otherness, as would be the alternate evaluation of masculinity and male sexuality. The penis and the uterus are merely signs for masculine power and feminine power; it is the power of the masculine assertion and feminine receptivity that is envied. Freud spoke of penis envy in the woman; Horney countered with womb envy in the man. The two metaphors are almost laughable because the symbols are far too meager to capture what Freud and Horney were attempting to convey. They lose their meaning altogether. Each theorist was, in his and her own way, attempting to image and recreate men's and women's awestruck experience of the self and the other, the profound differentness that each feels in relation to the other, and the desire to have what the other has. Horney and Freud were trying to contain in a word, in a body part, the immensity of the discovered other that one can never be. When one experiences envy, attempts to spoil the envied other, and fears retaliation from the other, then one is susceptible to shame.

The Evocation of Shame

Nathanson (1992) states that to know sex is to know shame (p. 300). To know deprivation is to know shame. To know oneself as unmanned, as womanish, as woman, as mannish is to know shame. Men denigrate women as a way to "avenge early rejection by the mother, [to] rebel against authority, [to express envy of women's private and ethical power, and to] devalue the primary object of dependency, [it is] the defensive denial by men of their own powerlessness" (Steven & Gardner, 1994, p. 139). Women become the containers for men's problem with the tenderness and aggression. Women devalue men as a way to avenge rejection and exploitation by the father, to express their envy of men's public and financial power, to devalue the primary object of independence. Men become containers for women's problem with solitude and enmeshment.

In summary, shame is evoked in relations between men and women in the following way: Each self identifies the other as a source of power; the power is in the fact of its Otherness. This identification of the other as powerful is a common unconscious reality. In facing that power, each feels terror and envy toward the other. As the man and the woman see in each other all that the self is not, each feels ashamed. The woman, for the sake of maintaining their connectedness, introjects her terror, envy, and shame; thus hiding herself. She feels sad. The man, for the sake of maintaining their separateness, projects his terror, envy, and shame onto or into her; thus, emptying himself. He feels mad. He blames her for his anger; she shames him for her sadness. She blames him for her hiding; he shames her for his emptiness. In order to make the otherness manageable it is reduced to identification as a body part. In attempting to remain in communion the woman and the man take steps to resolve their shame. That resolution most often seems to take the form of female and feminine voicelessness and male and masculine violence. There is another solution: The masculine in each person must hear the feminine into speech; and the feminine in each person must nourish the masculine into peace (Cook & Dworkin, 1992).[8]

Identifying the Interpersonal Sequences of the Shame Event

Shame may have a positive function of protecting one's privacy; or of safeguarding a relationship (Schneider, 1987). While shame is a painful affect, it may serve to restore balance to a human organism that is about to be overwhelmed. However, shame is also disgrace and dishonor (Berke, 1987; Kinston 1987; Schneider, 1987; Wursmer, 1987); it is felt as an assault on the self which threatens the self with psychic annihilation. Which kind of shame is experienced depends greatly on the other person involved and the circumstances of the involvement.

Since shame is essentially an interpersonal experience, it is especially likely to operate in close and intimate relationships. It is likely to be felt most deeply in the relationships which supply or ought to supply the most connectedness and care. It is likely to be the most wounding in the relationships in which people let their least acceptable selves be known. The radical dependency of human incapacity creates a proneness to shame; all responses to that self-limitedness evoke shame; the most rejecting or punitive responses evoke humiliation and rage.

Shame is a particular form of interpersonal behavior which may be expressed intrapsychically or interpersonally or both. The behavior can be described using terms from the SASB model that was introduced in Chapter 2. In its general form, the shame encounter occurs in six behavioral steps of an interpersonal communication system that I will describe from the point of view of the one who feels shame: (a) The creation of a connection, (disclosing, expressing, joyful connection, trusting, and/or relying [focus on self]); (b) the exposure event, which leads to an immediate self-consciousness expressed as deference and/or submission (focus on self); (c) the precipitate reorientation to watching the other, or the subversion of shame by immediate reversal to counterattack (focus on other); (d) the simultaneous orientation to the intrapsychic self-other interface, which will include self-attack, self-neglect, and/or self-indictment (focus on introject); (e) the other's response to the exposure, which will include watching, blaming, belittling, attacking, and/or rejecting (focus on other); and (f) the attempt to restore or to terminate the interpersonal connection (focus on self-other interface). The actual content of these encounters and the possibility of nonshaming responses from the other determine the exact course and resolution of the shame encounter.

The shame event is one in which many levels of awareness exist simultaneously. It is as if the individual were trying to watch many movie screens at once as they are playing all around the room. The loss of cognitive content and the inability to speak that is described by shame researchers may be due to perceptual, emotional, and cognitive overload that "short-circuits" the system (Tomkins, 1987; Nathanson, 1987). Thus, shame could be described as the person's cognitive-affective circuit-breakers which serve to protect the person-system from power surges. Certainly, there are myriad encounters that we could focus on. However, I will focus on only gendered relating. That is, I will describe social behaviors in which sexuality or genderality significantly contribute to the purpose and force of the encounters.

Punishment

Attacks on the self evoke shame (Cameron & Magaret, 1951). In simple shame situations, the self is criticized, blamed, and attacked by another person for some quality of their beingness which they cannot change (having blue eyes, for example); they sulk and recoil; they have just been shamed. In the more elaborated sequences, they will also self-blame and self-reject in response to the attack; they have also experienced a reciprocal reception of shaming. Cameron and Magaret describe such encounters in the course of the child's learning of the language for describing his or her sexual identity. Nathanson (1992) suggests the parents are ill-equipped to respond to or to describe children's sexual experience in ordinary, helpful, and nonshaming ways. For example: Nathanson reports that Puerto Rican parents would smile and laugh with pride at the sight of their son's erection, while an American mother reported profound embarrassment in response to her infant son's erection.

Lewis (1971) found that women often use shaming communications. This communication style in child-rearing may create a more complicated shaming response for males in relation to significant other women. Male's physiological limitations due to a variety of biological factors may impact their sense of efficacy and mastery that impact their sense of efficacy and mastery. Because of men's physiological limitations and the poor treatment they experience, males may develop a particular form of shame-proneness which they attempt to circumvent by projecting the shame in the form of denigration of the other (the powerful woman) or by spoiling her. When a man's dependency is exposed or is in danger of exposure, he feels ashamed. He projects the shame onto or into the woman; he feels humiliated rage, and lashes out in violence in order to get rid of the shame. The woman is punished for his feeling of deficiency and inferiority.

Mystification

Laing (1965) defines mystification in terms of the mystifier and the mystified. One who muddles, obscures, or masks is the mystifier; the one who is muddled or confused is the mystified. "One of the functions of mystification is to avoid authentic conflict" (p. 344), although conflict may be apparent and serve to mystify the source or purpose of the conflict. One form of mystification "confirm[s] the content of an experience and disconfirms its modality" (p. 345). The other type of mystification occurs "when one person disconfirms the content of the other's experience and replaces it by attributions of experience conjunctive with one's view of the other (p. 345). Of particular interest to this discussion of sexuality and genderality, he states that

Mystification is particularly potent when it involves [a] rights-obligations system in such a way that one person appears to have the right to determine the experience of another, or, complementarily, when one person is under an obligation to the other(s) to experience, or not to experience, himself, them, his world, or any aspect of it, in a particular way. (p. 346)

For Laing, if one hopes to demystify a relationship, one must require all members of the relationship to present and compare all perspectives on the "shared situation," and to establish the veracity and the validity of all perspectives. Often, individuals attribute illness or evil intent, "madness or badness," to others. Interpersonal interactions which focus on sexuality and genderality would be especially prone to sequences in which a subject is mystified because sexuality and genderality are so much conceived of as mutually exclusive beingness. This susceptibility highlights the need for men and women to develop "bi-genderality" in order to overcome the apperception of existential ontological otherness of living as concretely embodied, sexed beings.

Gilman (1882/1973) presents us with a particularly powerful example of mystification in her short story, *The Yellow Wallpaper*: A young married woman and her physician husband are spending the summer in the country. He tells her she is not sick, but treats her illness, "nervous exhaustion." She attempts to think about her own cure, but he says that thinking about the condition is the worst thing she can do. She asks for social concourse, but he believes it to be counterindicated. She asks for meaningful work, but he believes it to be counterindicated. She feels weaker and weaker in her constricted circumstances; she is moved to the room with yellow wallpaper. In her isolation she experiences the house as strange (estranged?) to her. The husband says it is a draught and closes the window. She takes pains to control herself so as not to irritate him, which makes her very tired. As her life's attention narrows to nothing but the wallpaper in her room, the patterns in the paper begin to come to life. She is more and more tired and listless, and wants to leave; he tells her that she is getting "better and better." She objects; he counters that it pleases her to be ill. She finds meaningful "work" eventually, pulling away the living wallpaper, in order to get out of the room that she cannot leave. She has found a way to be well, while she is sick, because she is well, so that she can be sick, so that he can be well. What a poignant depiction of someone who fulfils her obligation so that the other can exert his right to determine the experience of the one! Her madness is the resolution she finds for the shame of her/his extreme femininity (passivity), enforced by the inability to see her masculinity (capacity for work) as her, not his, own. Laing (1965) has identified the schizophrenogenic nature of such contradictory and paradoxical treatment, as has Hayley (1963). Chesler (1972) has examined the paradoxical and binding communications used with women by mental health professionals and has built a strong case for the iatrogenic and nosocomial nature of paradoxical and binding treatment that has existed historically in American psychotherapeutic practices with women. Treatment has focused on helping women "adjust" by becoming passive in relation to men while identifying passivity as a symptom of ill health (see Broverman et al., 1970, 1972).

A parallel process occurs with regard to men and their expression of masculinity. In the masculinity-making system described by Stevens and Gardner (1994), we can see denial and refusal of need in the adult American male as a parallel discourse on the madness that befalls one who is forced to be exclusively autonomous and, therefore, the competent, valuable, masculine male, but who is not exclusively autonomous nor always competent. More recently, Chesler (1978) has explored men's experience and has identified "father-son hostility" (p. xvii) as an important source of "primal guilt" (p. xvi) in men's experience. She points to a potent contradiction between historical accounts of men's activities in death dealing (war, homicide, genocide, infanticide) and men's activities of culture-building. She also highlights the ambivalence and wishfulness that men experience,[9] as depicted in cinema, with regard to their desire for "'good' father-son relationships: of mutual trust, respect, and protectiveness" (p. xvii). In the terms of this study and that of Fine-Thomas (1993), Chesler seems to be referring to men's experience of shame over their dangerous aggressiveness and their experience of ontic gender guilt over the correlation between aggression and maleness. Chester concludes that men's attempts at civilized behavior are a form of reaction formation (rather than sublimation, as Freud suggested) directed toward saving men from the experience of being irredeemably bound to a basic nature of annihilating aggression.

In the preceding discussion we have developed a portrayal of women's experience as bound by the paradoxes of cultural pressures regarding appropriate femininity in such a way that to be as they ought they must be not as they are: Active, creative and passive, receptive. On the other hand, men also experience cultural pressures to be as they are not: Aggressive, dominant and vulnerable-affectionate, submissive. These paradoxical and binding messages are communicated in the intense interpersonal arenas of the family in childhood, through the media, and by other significant adults in children's lives.[10] The culture's insistence that men be only masculine and that women be only feminine leaves men and women attempting to obey a fundamentally mystifying and maddening command. Women and men, boys and girls are left the same task facing the schizophrenic: to learn "to manipulate and confound the categories of doing and the categories of being" (Laing,1965, p. 37) in order to continue to exist intrapsychically and interpersonally because they cannot be what they are not, nor not be what they are.

Double-bind

Laing (1965) states that the concept of mystification and the double-bind concept (Bateson, Jackson, Haley, & Weakland, 1956) are overlapping but not synonymous. The double bind is a special case of mystification. The key difference is that the double bind leaves the bound one with only one "right" way to respond within the defining criteria of the system (Laing, 1965; Rotzien & Vande Kemp, 1989a). A classic example of the double bind is the command, "be spontaneous." To comply disallows spontaneity, by the definition of the word; to resist, which would satisfy the definition of "spontaneous," contradicts the rule of process that is shaped by the command.

The female protagonist in the story, *The Yellow Wallpaper* (Gilman, 1882/1973), was double bound as well as mystified. The boy who is told that he cannot have his own deficiencies and dependency needs while he in fact, has then is double bound. In these cases the double bind leads to feelings of self-watchfulness, self-attack, and self-distancing that are indicative of shame. Voicelessness, violence, and madness may follow close behind.

Projective Identification

Experiences of projective identification may lead to shame provoking and shame evoking responses. A Male's need to feel efficacious and masterful may lead him to attempt to circumvent the shame he feels over his dependency and limitedness by projecting them in the form of denigration of and contempt for the powerful woman. His dependency is exposed or is in danger of exposure; he feels ashamed. He projects the shame onto or into the woman; he feels humiliated rage, and lashes out in violence in order to get rid of the shame. The woman is punished for his feeling of deficiency and inferiority.

If the woman, in turn, receives the denigration, devaluation, and shame into her self-experience in such a way as to become them, this experience of shaming punishment becomes projective identification. In this case the woman would respond to the man as if the devaluation, denigration, and shame were her own, and in her person. Thus, she responds with introjective identification. The man and woman cooperate in blaming the woman as victim, because she is the terrible feminine that he cannot allow in himself. In the process the man's own victim nature would be lost from view. The reverse would lead the projective identification of the woman's masculinity into the man. It is also easy to imagine interpersonal interactions that are constructed to achieve projective identification of a man's masculinity into a woman or a woman's femininity into a man. Jungian discourse provides a useful language for discussing such cases. Terms such as "masculine ego," "feminine ego," "anima," and "animus" help to separate the various intrapsychic and interpersonal dynamics that contribute to these complicated interpersonal behaviors.

Voicelessness and Violence

It has become clear how the shaming of genderality and sexuality occurs. Self-enforced voicelessness and violence are individuals' attempts to escape the shaming conditions of the shaming environments in which individuals feel imprisoned. The appearance of imprisonment is due to the concretization of masculine and the feminine traits in male and the female biologies, respectively. This points us back to the necessity to carefully disentangle the embodied sexuality of human experience from the personological genderality which is not confined to or assigned by biology. Only men may be men, and only women may be women. However, women may be masculine and feminine, and men may be feminine and masculine.

Conclusion

Women are shamed for behaving in masculine ways, for being aggressive and dominant. Women are also shamed for behaving in feminine ways, for being demure and submissive. By traditional prescriptions that match gender to sex, a woman may be valued, for her receptivity and passivity but not for her assertiveness or initiative. Men, on the other hand, may be biologically predisposed to dominant aggressive (but not necessarily hostile) behavior, and they are trained to express aggression and dominance while being punished for expressing weakness and passivity (especially in relations with other men).

Women and girls are punished, humiliated, and belittled for behaving in masculine and feminine ways. Men and boys are punished, humiliated, and belittled for behaving in feminine ways; they are punished and rewarded (depending on situational variables) for expressing extreme forms of aggression, such as fighting and warring, and for less hostile but socially descriptive aggression, such as slamming doors or physically intruding on teachers, parents, or sibling. Significant adults' humiliating, coercive and punishing reactions to children's gendered behaviors, feelings, and thoughts cause children to feel shame in both its forms: constraint, modesty or shyness and dishonor or disgrace (Schneider, 1987; Wurmser, 1987).

As modesty or shyness, shame functions to protect the interface of the public and the private spheres (Nathanson, 1992). Since men's roles and women's roles have often been designated in terms of the split between these two realms, with women having responsibility for the private, it is not surprising that women are more prone to experience shame. Historically men have protected the home from external incursion while women have protected the relationships within the home. According to Schneider (1987) and Wurmser (1987) shame serves this protective function well. Shame also protects the individual's personal private boundaries by turning down or turning off pleasure that may either overwhelm or expose. This type of shame may be experienced in the presence of an other but not necessarily evoked by the interpersonal behavior of the other (Nathanson, 1992).

However, shame can also be experienced as disgrace or dishonor. In such instances, shame is evoked in interpersonal situations that involve aggression, defeat, failure and/or disappointment; shame is evoked by the humiliating and belittling behavior of the important other that is expressed toward the child or adult (Lewis, 1971). Shame and evocation of shame may serve to sever relatedness and connection. When experienced as rage and condemnation by a significant other, shame may annihilate the sense of self and self-esteem.

Shame may be induced systematically in the service of teaching children what is inappropriate social behavior. When shaming occurs routinely in relation to sex and gender, individuals become especially vulnerable to the pathological consequences of shame (which include voicelessness, avoidance and violence) because sexuality and genderality are experienced as part of existential and ontological beingness.

Men, women girls, and boys experience humiliating and belittling attacks on their personhood through the processes of punishment, mystification, double binding, and projective identification, and they feel ashamed. Awareness of the "otherness" that is concretely represented by sex differences evokes feelings of self-consciousness and jealousy. When sexuality and genderality are punished they become associated with feelings of worthlessness, failure, and defectiveness which provoke shame. In attempts to avoid the hostility of significant others or to avoid wanting parts of one's self-experience that are prohibited by the other, shame serves to interrupt the pleasure evoked by experiencing one's sexuality and genderality. Individuals become self-watchful and self-critical in an effort to avoid the proscribed behaviors so that they will not be the despised feminine as they are accused of being by significant others.

Shame is a very powerful mechanism of social control. When a strong, significant, and valued person belittles and humiliates another person, he or she has a great deal of interpersonal power over the other. The connection between shame and interpersonal power will be explored in Chapter 5.

As I have pursued this exploration, I have been troubled by repeated thoughts that this discussion does not include much reflection on the shame that is related to class and racial features of personal and interpersonal experience. Morrison (1992) speaks of the African American character in American fiction as being created by the author as the "serviceable other." As I mentioned at the end of Chapter 3, all those who succeed, all or partly, in becoming the supremely valued Masculine Other[11] will be able to recreate all non-masculine (and also feminine) others as objectified serviceable others who are perceived as having no subjective experience to be considered. As Laing (1965) commented, the only way out of this mystification is through a deliberate commitment to identify, to explore, and to validate all points of view. It is very important to understand here, that to validate is not the same as to verify. To verify is an action that depends on perception, cognition and rules of logic; verification takes the evidence, weighs it, and determines the *factuality* of the matter at hand. To validate, on the other hand, is an action that depends on affection, will and values; validation takes the process and the persons, holds them, and determines the *significance* of the matter and the persons at hand.

To some extent gender differences are limited and delimited by class and race differences. Many men and women are nonwhite and poor. Blue-collar males care for the material world in ways that are more similar to women's caregiving than to the work done by upperclass, hierarchs as they name and order the world and its care providers. All of the "others," in relation to culture's Masculinity, will experience shame at the exposure of their not-Masculinity, and, also, of their Femininity. The reverse is true as well: From the subjective perspective of the nonmasculine groups, the Masculine Other becomes the "serviceable other" over and against whom the nonmasculine subject can create its own name. To the extent that they voice their names and labels, they can use it to evoke shame in the Masculine Other (see Sampson, 1993). To the extent that they objectify their objectifier, they will be unable to demystify the mystification, to untie the double bind to prevent a simple bind from being doubled, or to refuse to introject a prospective identification.

Although race and class difference has been acknowledged in this study, these categories of difference and the experience of their members in relation to shame have not been adequately explored. Thus, how other racial, social, and economic groups are, how they are affected by, and how they affect the culture in relation to masculinity and femininity is less clear, and must be explored at another time.

Chapter 5.
Power and Gender

> "[Aaron] shall cast lots upon the two goats ... the goat, on which the lot fell to be the scapegoat, shall be presented alive before the Lord to make atonementwith him, and to let him go for a scapegoat into the wilderness ... [he shall]confess over him all the iniquities of the children of Israel ... and the goat shall bear upon him all the iniquities unto a land not inhabited: and he shall let go the goat in the wilderness."
>
> Leviticus 16:8, 10, 21, 22 (KJV)

> "...much more the members of the body which seem to be more feeble are necessary ... those members of the body which we think to be less honorable, upon these we bestow more abundant honor ... Whether one member suffers, all the members suffer with it, or one member be honored, all members rejoice with it."
>
> I Corinthians 12:22, 23, 26 (KJV)

> "Submitting yourselves one to another in the fear of God."
>
> Ephesians 5:21 (KJV)

Shame is a powerful affect or emotion that functions to dampen or extinguish interest, pleasure, and/or excitement. According to Nathanson (1992), proto-shame occurs spontaneously in infancy in order to interrupt the infant's engagement with an object, a situation, or, especially, a person. As interpersonal experience accumulates, the infant comes to know that certain intensely enjoyable experiences are disapproved of by the mother or the father or some other important adult. In moments of intense pleasure that have become associated with the adult's negating response, the child learns to shut off the pleasure with shame in order to avoid the adult's displeasure.[1] Thus, avoidance serves to maintain the positive interpersonal connection with the significant adult.

If the adult not only rejects or prohibits the child's pleasurable experience, but also ridicules or humiliates the child's being in the experience, the child will feel dishonoring shame. If the adult attacks features of the child's self experience that are fundamental to its nature, the more likely it is that the shame will become associated with the child's sense of self, and the more likely it is that the child will come to experience itself as fundamentally and irredeemably flawed. Two categories of the child's self experience which often receive adult belittling and humiliation are sexuality and genderality; expression of femininity is especially likely to be attacked. When adult attacks on the child's vulnerability occur, the child loses control over the other, the self, and its own sense of value and becomes powerless.[2] This view of the self as powerless may be carried intrapsychically throughout life as a harsh and punitive introject (the superego) and as an inner demand to become perfect (an unattainable ego-ideal).

Power is "the ability to act or produce an effect" (*Merriam-Webster's Collegiate Dictionary*, 1993, p. 913), and it always part of every relationship; power resides in every person in every relationship. Sexuality and genderality are a part of that power, and it is because of their power that they are so attractive and because of the attraction that they are so powerful. It is also because of their power that they hold such a great potential to evoke shame. French (1985), in *Beyond Power*, suggests that we must "feminize" the world. On the contrary, we must feminine-ize *and* masculine-ize the world; that is, we must acclaim *and* lay claim to human connectedness *and* human separateness, to independence *and* to mutual dependence, to invincibility *and* to vulnerability. Shaming of femininity (interpersonal connection) and aggrandizement of negative masculinity (hostile aggression) must cease. The discipline of psychology is beginning to emphasize gendered wholeness in descriptions of human personality (Blass & Blatt, 1992; Blatt & Blass, 1990; Guisinger & Blatt, 1994). Developmentalists, psychoanalysts, and philosophers are recognizing the need to incorporate connection and separateness and independence and mutual dependence in accounts of the personality and the development of the self and social roles. Acknowledgment of the need for connection and interdependence as well as for separateness and independence will influence understandings and definitions of power (Cushman, 1990; Sampson, 1993).

Power has often been defined primarily in terms of hostile dominance and competition (French, 1985), behaviors that are described in the SASB model by the left side of the Other surface—belittling and blaming, attacking and rejecting, ignoring and neglecting. This understanding of power is based on an assumption that the dominator may act in determining ways with regard to a submissive other, and the submissive other must respond with compliance as determined by the dominator. Determining behavior could be described by terms found on the upper halves of the Focus on Self and Focus on Other surfaces of the SASB model (expressions of independence), and the submissive other would respond in a complementary and opposite ways with behaviors described in the bottom halves (expressions of dependence). These behaviors are especially potent in coercing compliance when they are hostile and threaten or inflict injury. In such situations, all freedom is in the hands of the dominator; thus, power is equated with freedom from constraint. French (1985) suggests a need for members of western culture is to transcend this kind of power. She states that "[f]eminism is the only serious, coherent, and universal philosophy that offers an alternative" (p. 442) to domination. She continues by asserting the value of the feminine (by which she seems to mean "women") and proceeds along the course she has set to the conclusion: Feminizing the world is needed in order to save it. However, the feminine is not all good, nor is the masculine all bad. Further, simply adding women to public institutions and discourse will not solve the ills of the world; women are as good and as bad as men, and men as well as women may behave in feminine ways. Although simply adding women and femininity is not the solution, French and a growing number of others are correct in calling attention to the fact that hostile dominance is not good for anyone. Leary (1957) has pointed out that hostile behavior—identified by the SASB model as sulking and scurrying, recoiling and protesting, walling off and distancing, belittling and blaming, attacking and rejecting, and ignoring neglecting—is generally considered pathological. The human qualities of joy, peace, patience, kindness, generosity, fidelity, gentleness, and self-control (all of which are identified by the SASB model as friendly and affiliative) often have been associated with femininity. A new kind of power tactics would include mutual determination—including those qualities of rationality and validation that Laing (1965) referred to in his description of demystification. Codetermined power (mutual and independent as opposed to other-determinedand and unilateral) is needed.

Power and the Structural Analysis of Social Behavior

Hayley (1986) understands power as the ability to influence another person's behavior. As Hayley uses the concept of power, a person has achieved power when he has established himself as the one to determine what is going to happen. Power tactics are those maneuvers a person uses to give himself influence and control over his social world and so to make that world more predictable. Defined thus broadly, a man has power if he can order someone to behave in a certain way, but he also has power if he can provoke someone to behave that way. (pp. 37–38)

Hoffman (1981) suggests that power lies in having control of access. Rausch (1965) states that individuals attempt to gain power through moral persuasion (appeal) or harassment (coercion), so power has to do with relative degrees of independence. According to Carson (1969), interpersonal power is the ability to elicit complementary responses to one's own actions. Carson's definition is:

Complementarity occurs on the basis of reciprocity in respect to the dominance-submission axis (dominance tends to induce submission, and vice versa), and on the basis of correspondence in respect to the hate-love axis (hate induces hate, and love induces love). (p. 112)

In addition to complementarity, Carson used two other terms: noncomplementarity, a response in which "a person accepts only one of the two components defined by the axes of the circle"; and anticomplementarity, a response in which a person rejects both components of the initiator's bid for reciprocity" (Okiyama, 1989, p. 57). These responsive behaviors would shift communication from the level of trading verbal content to the level of discussing what content is allowed and how it will be discussed.

Dominant Power and Codetermined Power

Delgado (1989) and Okiyama (1989) have investigated the relationship between complementarity and status. Persons of high status are admired, imitated, and deferred to by the low status person. Status is assigned according to two sets of factors: by virtue of fortuitous factors such as age, sex, birth, complexion, race; and by virtue of the individual's accomplishments. Delgado investigated complementarity, looking at the relationship between hostile-dominance and hostile-submission using the SASB model and methods, and found that hostile-submission occurs as a complement to an initiating behavior of hostile-dominance. He also found that controlling behavior followed in response to hostile-submission. Okiyama (1989), also using the SASB model and methodology, investigated the impact of status on complementarity. (In Chapter 2, the SASB model was described; one additional definition will be necessary: The *antithesis* is the opposite of the complement of a given communication behavior.

For example, the behavior is attacking , its complement is recoiling , and the opposite of recoiling is joyfully connecting.)

Okiyama (1989) found that, in response to antecedent behaviors: High status individuals used more complementary responses than low status individuals, high status individuals used antithesis more often in response to hostile than to friendly behaviors; and high status individuals used friendly dominance more than they used any other cluster of responses. In addition, low status individuals were more likely to focus on self, and were less likely to respond to self-focus antecedents with complementary other-focus; that is, low-status individuals are not likely to give attention to another's self-focused communication. Low status individuals complement other-focus antecedent behavior with their own self-focus responses, while higher status individuals complement self-focus antecedent behaviors of low status individuals with other-focus. The higher status individuals complemented disclosing with affirmation , joyful connection with approaching , and submission with controlling, and they affirmed autonomy. Lower status individuals used antithesis, separating to respond to nurturing, and distancing to respond to controlling behaviors, while high status individuals used antithesis, controlling to asserting, and affirming to sulking. High status individuals used affirmation in response to blaming. Okiyama (1989) concluded that "[o]perationalization of status as Focus on Other relative to Focus on Self has heuristic value" (p. 26).

Okiyama suggests that the use of complementarity, noncomplementarity, antithesis, and nonhostile response to hostile dominance are due to the high status individual having access to more resources than the low status individual. Implied is that the high status person has a responsibility as well as a capacity to make better and broader use of those relational resources. Okiyama states that hostile behavior is not socially desirable, but low status individuals may not have alternative skills for resolving conflict. Hostile aggression is a complex behavior that is likely to evoke hostile responses. In order to achieve more harmonious and cooperative human relationships, more accurate and sophisticated understandings of the sources of aggression are needed so that better training in conflict resolution can occur. Descriptions of aggression and training individuals in alternative conflict resolution skills need to take into account the fact that aggression is thought to have biological as well as environmental determinants.

However, there is a good deal of debate as to how expression of aggression is determined by biological and environmental factors

(Jacklin, 1989; Maccoby; 1990; Miedzian, 1991; Moir & Jessell, 1991; Pleck, 1981). While the report of sex differences in the expression of aggressive behavior is one of the most reliable findings in the literature on sex difference, there is controversy as to the meaning of the observed differences. First, many studies of aggression report a good deal of within group variation as well as the between group variation. Second, "aggression" is operationalized differently from study to study. Often, "aggression" designates simply high levels of gross motor activity, distractibility, and interference with classroom procedures (a set of behaviors typically found in Attention Deficit Disorder, a syndrome that affects boys with far greater frequency than girls). In other studies "aggression" means fighting, and other forms of physical violence. Violence is increasingly reported to be of major concern to the American Public ("For teens," 1995). How can society and its institutions decrease the incidence of hostile aggression and increase cooperation? Why is hostile aggression a predominantly male problem? Gardner and Stevens (1994) suggest that American men are violent because they were forced into too much independence much too soon and because their physical limitations have not been adequately diagnosed and treated. Men may come to rely on hostile dominance as their only means to effect change because they despair of achieving any other kind of power.

Use and Abuse of Power

Power is the ability to be effective or to influence others. Abusive power (hostile dominance) is detrimental to the well-being of an other or others. It may be action taken with a conscious or deliberate attempt to inflict injury, or it may be unconscious or inadvertent action which causes harm. The primary focus of the powerful person is on some effect that is satisfying to the powerful one.

Hayley (1986) suggests that provocation of a response is as much an expression of power as is the ability to command a response. Command is direct; provocation is indirect. Take for instance this example based on the work Satir (1967), a husband and wife are going to dinner, but the wife is more tired than hungry:

She: Where do you want to eat?

He: I don't care.

She: I don't care either; where do you want to go?

They are at an impasse. The wife could say, "you choose," a direct command. Instead she becomes agitated tearful, and whiny.

She: You never tell me what you want; you're so hard to please!

He (with frustration): I really don't care. How about Chinese?
She (sobbing): You know I'm allergic to MSG
He storms out of the room, shouting: I'm not hungry!
She stops crying, takes a shower and goes to bed.

The wife did not want to go out, but could not simply say so (she feels powerless because of various rules against women's direct speech) but she was able to communicate her reluctance indirectly in such a way that provoked her husband to make the choice of her desire (because of rules allowing or even requiring that men decide and speak). The husband has expressed power in effecting an end to the discussion, but has done so in a hostile and disaffiliating way. This couple behaved in a complementary way to achieve a resolution to their dinner problem, but they were unable to function in a way that was mutually accountable for a mutually beneficial outcome. He must order, and she must provoke. (A more effective communication would have interrupted the content in order to assess the process of engagement.) In more mutual and reciprocal relationships, each member would have access to a variety of power tactics that would be used to negotiate and effect outcomes. Further, they would share and trade access, control, and resources (Hoffman, 1981). In healthy human relations, power is likely to be expressed by moral persuasion rather than by coercion, in order to maintain mutual interdependence and individual independence (Rausch, 1965). According to Carson's (1969) definition of power, mutuality and codetermination would be evidenced by shifts from situation to situation in who is dominant and who is submissive; health and maturity would be evidenced by the predominance of loving exchanges rather than hateful ones. Abusive power is used to coerce one person in a relationship to function according to the needs of another without regard for the needs of the nondominant person, and may be expressed directly or indirectly, in commanding or in provocative ways.

Alternately, I propose the term "codetermined power" to indicate a coordinated and mutual application of individual and shared capacities in order to bring about mutually desired and mutually agreed upon effects. The expression of codetermined power depends fundamentally on mutually constrained freedom and consensus decision-making processes. Each participant is viewed as an agent and as a dependent; each perspective must be taken as information of common concern; action plans must be mutually satisfactory. In relationships based on codetermined power, behavior implemented to meet goals will likely be diverse; and social behavior of the participants during implementation will not be rigidly complementary nor rigidly symmetrical (Watzlawick, Beavin, & Jackson, 1967). Interpersonal communication will likely include complementarity, noncomplementarity, and anticomplementarity, as well as antitheses and opposition, but it will not display high levels of hostile behaviors. According to research done by Maccoby (1990) and her colleagues, a style similar to this description of codetermined power is more typical of women and girls than of boys. Little boys are more likely to express influence (i. e., power) through the use of direct commands and self assertions. Why little boys are less inclined to cooperation and mutual care is unclear from the available data, but has been linked to their disidentification with the mother by some theorists (Chodorow, 1978; Stevens & Gardner, 1994).

Displays of abusive power will include high levels of rigid complementarity in which one person usually dominates while the other usually submits. Forms of power that rely heavily on dominance, aggression, and hostility have been associated with masculinity (Chodorow, 1978; French, 1985). These forms of power may easily give rise to shaming encounters in which the submissive individual is belittled, attacked, and neglected in order to coerce him or her into behaving in the way that the powerful person desires. The story in Chapter 4 of the little boy who was bullied by his father into not crying is an example of being coerced to act "not like a girl" so as to escape the shame evoked by the big person's rage.

Feminine Power and Masculine Power

Power is not only abusive, competitive hostile-dominance, nor is power simply masculine and the prerogative of males. However, these associations of power with maleness and masculinity have contributed to current understandings of power. Following from the discussion of gender and its confounds in Chapter 2, we can describe and clarify the concepts of feminine and masculine power. Feminine power has been more difficult to see because it is performed less publicly, less overtly, and less directly. In the past, the feminine has been confounded with mothering, with female biology, and with the private sphere. Feminine power is found in such acts as receptivity, holding and enfolding, connection, and tending (Josselson, 1992). These features of the feminine are positive to the extent that they create security, nurturance, and trust; however, they may be negative if they clutch, suffocate, and/or overwhelm. In the past, sometimes feminine power has influenced public life when it has been expressed by those who have private access to commanding, public people. For, example, the media have portrayed Nancy Reagan and Barbara Bush as very powerful because they shared private lives with U.S. presidents. These women, although not having direct access to expressions of power in the public arena, were portrayed as wielding considerable persuasive and provocative power in private. When Bill Clinton became president, he and his wife challenged U. S. citizens, unsuccessfully, to acknowledge and allow a president's wife to wield her personal power publicly, and relatively independently from her president-husband who is in a command position, in his domain. I believe that the opposition to Mrs. Clinton's health care plan was at least in part a rejection of the interpersonal processes used in establishing her power. Some object to a woman and wife having overt, rather than covert, power. Some object to the First Lady's power becoming visible, while others object to her use of private power as a means to gain access to public command.

Masculine power is found in such acts as penetration, standing alone, separating, and extending. These features are positive to the extent that they create ways and means, action, agency, and productivity; however, they may be negative if they intrude, isolate, coerce, and/or destroy. An example of positive masculine power is the capacity to react speedily in a crisis to initiate remedies and to act assertively, in order to direct attention and resources to the appropriate places so that the crisis is resolved. An example of negative masculine power is the use of aggression to force an individual to engage in unwanted sexual behaviors. Let me repeat the caution: This is not a discussion about men in power versus women in power. This is a description of qualities or characteristics of the human personality. Masculine and feminine features of personality exist in women; feminine and masculine features exist in men. In western culture, achieving women have had to become skilled in the use of masculine power, and some people have worried that women will stop being feminine. Some men have acquired the skills of nuturance and care, and some people are worried that men will lose their masculinity. However, masculinity and femininity are not mutually exclusive. Each source of power may create, and each may destroy. Each may give voice, and each may do violence.

Aggressive and assertive dominance has been associated with masculinity and has been a part of human experience throughout history. Dominance has been a primary method for effecting change in the public sphere. Cooperative and caring relatedness have been associated with femininity and also has been a part of human experience throughout history. Relatedness has been a primary method for effecting change in the private sphere. Increasing attention is being paid to violence and means to control it. So far, that attention is being directed toward some of the most obvious forms of violence that are being committed by the most deprived segments of human society, such as the gang violence of poor members of the urban ghetto. It remains to be seen whether attention will become directed toward more subtle and more socially accepted forms of violence, such as the exploitive competitive work practices that force many out of the workplace or the abusive and exploitive atmosphere created by media violence and materialism. Several psychologists (Cushman, 1990; Guisinger & Blatt, 1994; Sampson, 1993) have suggested that a major shift may be occurring in western cultural understandings of human nature, that there is mounting evidence that supports the positive value of femininity (relatedness) and highlights the negative value of abusive masculinity (hostile dominance) which may give rise to a paradigm shift. The fact of relatedness as an ongoing part of human character and the recognition of the need for relatedness in human dealings are gaining currency. Whether individuals and institutions are able to refrain from shaming expressions of femininity (relatedness, the need for relatedness, the recognition of human vulnerability, and the need for protection and care) and to value, support, and foster the formation of positive expressions of femininity remains to be seen. This study will conclude with brief explorations of relatedness as it is expressed in two important social institutions, the family and the practice of psychotherapy.

Power, Gender, and the Family

Developmental research of adolescent identity formation highlights the need for positive interpersonal connection during the process of adolescents' differentiation from the family. It is interesting that this connection arises from the family itself. Grotevant and Cooper (1986) demonstrated convincingly that adolescents who achieve healthy autonomy do so in the context of supportive, caring, encouraging family members who are able to tolerate (or even teach) difference, to allow exploration, and to foster collegiality. Alternately, parental hostility may contribute to self-directed hostility in adolescents. Kaslow, Wamboldt, Wamboldt, and Anderson (1989) used the SASB model to identify the negative effects of parental complex messages of subtle hostility on a teenager's suicidality. Parents' simultaneous expressions of hostile control and hostile autonomy were perceived by their teenage daughter as direct attack which was introjected as self-attack expressed as suicidal thoughts and behaviors.

One interesting feature of their report is that fathers in these autonomy-generating families have significant positive influence on their children's development. What is significant about this finding is that it provides data that suggest that at least some fathers are and have been involved with their children's development, and it provides balance to findings that stress the importance of the mother. Though one could argue, as do the analytic schools (Gooch & Noble, 1989), that the mother's role take precedence during infancy and early childhood and that the father becomes more important only at later stages, I would counter that this is unexamined bias that has not been empirically demonstrated. Until recently, fathers have been extremely uninvolved with infants and toddlers (Brazelton, 1988; Chodorow, 1978; Mahler, 1975), and since the industrial revolution, fathers have been absent from the home as well as uninvolved in direct care of children. While there may be hormonal influences on tendencies to engage in childcare (Nathanson, 1992), arguments using these "firmwired" tendencies to explain father noninvolvment and father absence are not convincing. The arguments rest on one or both of two possible assumptions: (a) Human biological factors has a simple causal relationship to expressed human behavior that are far removed from each other in time and physiology; or (b) mothers should care for infants and children, while fathers should not.

Eurich-Rascoe (1988) reviewed the periodical literature of the impact of the father-daughter relationship on daughters' identity formation. A computerized review searching fathers and daughters yielded 25 articles published in the years 1974 to 1988. Of those articles 20 reported on father-daughter incest, and almost all articles reported on adult adjustment, measured as marital satisfaction, operationalized as self-reported contentment or happiness in the married state. In most studies fathers were available to their daughters as sexual partners, and most studies reported that the presence of father-daughter sexual relatedness was correlated with maladjustment in adulthood. Johnson (1986) concluded that men are now being encouraged to be more like mothers and that fathers' concern and feeling of responsibility for their daughters may be the best protection against incest and social withdrawal. But, she concluded, the data regarding fathers' influence on childrens' development is still limited. Hetherington and Deur (1971) found that father absence is usually associated with other disruptions in family life and is correlated with disturbance in the social and cognitive development of children. These negative outcomes can be mitigated by mothers' competence, as well as the by the presence of alternate male role models. It appears that the development of healthy masculinity in boys may be associated with father presence, and father absence is associated with increased femininity in sons in some studies.

Hetherington and Deur do not identify the influence of father presence on the daughters' development of masculinity. Phares (1992) reviewed the literature to answer the question "Where's Poppa?" and concluded that fathers' influence on children's development has not been well investigated due to four interrelated factors: participant recruitment is more difficult; parental pathology influences outcomes differentially; theories of development are sex-biased; and research assumptions are based on outmoded norms. More recent findings (Smith, 1995; Snarey, 1994) suggest that fathers' involvement with children throughout childhood have a strong influence on childrens' growth and adjustment. Snarey (1994) reported that fathers who encourage behavior contrary to sex-role stereotypes have a significant influence on children developing broad cross-gendered skills. Miller (1987) suggested with regard to harsh father involvement: "Children are faced with a tormentor they love, not one they hate" (p. 119). Perhaps, future research on nurturant fathering will give us more hopeful alternatives.[3]

Swigart (1991) has criticized theories of and research on mothering as being dominated by adults' childish fantasies of the "Good Fairy" and the "Evil Witch". She states, "At present, most of us in this culture identify so closely with children we forget we are the adults who must provide constant care for them" (p. 240). She argues that mothers have been given all responsibility for children's well-being with limited resources to achieve optimal outcomes. She states that mothers and mothering are idealized and devalued simultaneously and that the real experiences and needs of mothers have not been considered. In the family, parents have responsibility for the maturation of children. That parents' power over their children is limited is also true. Children are shaped by a variety of social influences, such as siblings, teachers, neighbors, peers, and the media. Educators, and trainers, and therapists for parents need to recognize all the various influences on children. Parents are powerful people in the lives of their children; and they need help to wield that power well. Without appropriate personal, economic, and institutional resources, parents are in a powerful position in the lives of their children, but they are disempowered. In this country expectations for success are high, and this expectation affects child-rearing as well. When expectations are high and resources are low, there is increased incidence of failure in parenting and marriage which increases the potential for the evocation of shame. Lansky (1987, 1992) indicates that paternal shame over perceived paternal and marital failure is a primary factor in family dysfunction and increased domestic violence is one outcome. Cooperative relatedness is needed by all family members; the role of femininity and who expresses it in the family must be reevaluated.

Parents must be helped to discover and to develop and to positively value their own femininity as well as masculinity. Parents are powerful people in the lives of their children; and they need help to wield that power well. They must have help in minimizing their own tendencies to resort to hostile dominance as a primary means of social control. A host of social institutions in the United States have responsibility to provide support, education and intervention in order that members of families will become more stable and healthy, having more interpersonal resources for the expression of autonomy and relatedness, masculinity and femininity, in service of children's growth and parents' productivity. One such institution is the discipline of psychology, especially psychotherapy.

Power, Gender, and the Practice of Psychotherapy

There has been an ongoing feminist critique of the practice of psychotherapy as it relates to women. The primary focus of this critique is that reliance on male-biased theories of women's psychology and of child development have made psychotherapy unuseful, and even harmful, to women. The same critique could be offered with regard to current treatmentof men as well, because inadequate understandings of women and children lead to misrepresenting men and their experience of women and children. The practice of psychotherapy has been affected in much the same way as other areas of the discipline of psychology. According to some observers in the field (Alpert, 1978; Torrey, 1987; Yoder & Kahn, 1993) male-biased theories have been supplemented by woman-added theories, and then supplanted by woman-biased theories. At this time the field is probably dominated by male-biased and woman-added thought, with some woman-biased thought being tenaciously espoused or tentatively explored. Psychologists are just now beginning to be evaluate human experience by a broader standard than male-biased, woman-added, and woman-biased standards (Cushman, 1990; Guisinger & Blatt, 1994; Sampson, 1993).

In the meantime, women may experience iatrogenic therapeutic failure: Women don't get "better" because the basic assumptive goal is for women and children to adapt to a fundamental cultural dysfunction. As a result women and children may be especially susceptible to harmful double bind and paradoxical communication that is intentionally or unintentionally inserted into the treatment by unwitting but biased, or by exploitive, practitioners. Women and children are more likely to be clients; in the past men have been less likely to seek treatment. Psychologists and other counselors would probably be explain this differential use of services by the "fact" that women present with symptoms, while men don't. Men come to the expert when the wife or the child needs to be fixed. Practitioners of the discipline have cooperated with men in identifying women and children as patients by emphasizing occupational functioning as the measure of men's adjustment and social and emotional functioning as the measure of women's adjustment without evaluating the circumstances in which those functions arise. Underlying the therapist-husband collusion is the practitioner's assumption that definitions of health that emphasize autonomy and lack of relatedness are accurate and good. The therapist assumes further that women must adjust themselves to role-expectations that are at odds with a positive valuing autonomy and disconnection and a negative valuing of interpersonal connection. However, they do not evaluate the values nor the shaming effect that the values have on women. In so doing, therapists expect women to maintain their role as the emotional one for the marital relationship which leaves women responsible for an area of shared experience over which they has no control: men's emotional life.

Another difficulty that exists for women as clients in current practices of psychotherapy is that women in therapy with male therapists are at risk of being exploited and discriminated against sexually and emotionally. I will deal only with the issue of emotional exploitation and discrimination here. If male therapists have not adequately examined their personal and professional biases and have adopted male-biased, woman-absent, woman-added, or woman-biased theories of development and therapeutic technique, then they will not be able to treat women adequately or ethically. One of the most significant problems with this kind of uninformed treatment is the therapists' inability to help the patient resolve what Lewis (1971) calls "unanalyzed shame" (p. 13) in relation to her understanding of her sexuality and genderality. This shame is both brought with the client who has a potent ego ideal regarding her functioning as a woman, in masculine and in feminine ways, and it is created by the treatment because the therapist (due to his potent unexamined and unresolved sex and gender biases) misattributes causes and effects to the woman's character, rather than to the social and interpersonal environment in which the woman finds herself. The therapist is in a higher status position vis-à-vis the female client due to the fortuitous factor of being male and due to the therapist's education and expertise. The female client is culturally conditioned to be compliant with males and with experts, and she attempts to relate to the psychotherapist according to this rule of appropriate social and feminine behavior. If the therapist has not evaluated his own commitment to the social rule prescribing lower-status, female compliance, he will not be able to help the client do so. Further, when she begins to discover the dysfunctionality of her compliance and attempts to address it in treatment, the male therapist may feel threatened due to his perception that she is criticizing the competence of his treatment. If he responds in defensive ways, he may punish the client or withdraw or begin to critique the changes in her behavior. To the extent that the client has developed an attachment to the therapist she is vulnerable to experience the therapist's nonsupportive or hostile reactions as attacking and she will introject them as self-blame. The therapist's attack and the client's self-attack are likely to provoke shame in the client. She may attempt to return to her more compliant behavior, but her increased self-awareness makes that return unsatisfactory. She may make attempts to discuss the therapeutic process, but it is likely that the therapist's continued reactivity will silence her, either due to her care for and loyalty to him or due to her acceptance of his determination that her noncompliant behavior is the problem. She is then doubly shamed: She feels shame in relation to herself because she cannot fundamentally comply with the treatment because it violates her new self-awareness , and she feels shame in relation to the significant-other-therapist because she is being inappropriate in his estimation by her noncompliance.

Three recent studies using SASB to investigate psychotherapy process identify client and therapist behaviors that affect treatment. Benjamin (1987a, 1987b) has described aspects of narcissistic and borderline functioning in interpersonal terms. In the case of self-mutilating behavior, she identifies the following sequence of behaviors: In an interpersonal encounter the client experiences perceived abandonment, devalues the abandoning other, withdraws from the social context, self-abandons intrapsychically, mutilates some body part, and feels relief. Often the client's family history contains repeated experiences of abandonment and a requirement that the client remain loyally connected to the family. Mutilation becomes a means for expressing the familial abandonment while maintaining the connection. This dynamic is bound to occur in the therapeutic context, and unexamined sex and gender biases in the therapist will make it more likely for the client to experience real emotional and cognitive abandonment by the therapist as she explores her genderality and sexuality. While Benjamin does not identify shame explicitly in her description of this process, the mechanisms of shame are obvious in the self-abandonment, the social withdrawal, and the self-attack. In another study, Henry, Schact, and Strupp (1990) explore the effects of therapist behaviors on treatment outcome. In their study poor outcomes were correlated with three aspects of therapist interpersonal behavior: (a) Therapist interpersonal behaviors confirmed the client's negative introject; (b) therapist subtly hostile and/or controlling statements were positively correlated with client statements of self-blame; and, (c) therapists with dissaffiliative introjects tended to engage in problematic interpersonal processes that have been associated with poor outcomes. These findings do not address genderality or sexuality specifically or explicitly, but they do suggest intriguing possibilities for the empirical investigation of interpersonal gendered and sexual behaviors and the impact of therapist evaluations of and reactions to them. From these data it is clear that the therapist's evaluations of various aspects of genderality might have a significant impact on the client's resolution of her own experience.

The therapists' valorization of masculine and feminine will also have a powerful impact on male clients' attempts to identify, evaluate, and develop healthy genderality. Therapists who are uncomfortable with male expressions of tenderness and other feminine qualities will react interpersonally in ways that will discourage, or shame, those expressions. The less aware and the less mature (and androgynous) the therapist is the less able the client will be to identify and practice those new roles. Just as adolescents need a supportive and open family environment in order to explore various roles, so to the client needs to be supported and not shamed in exploring and practicing new ways of being. Clients will be hindered in adopting their full femininity (the capacity for relatedness) and their full masculinity (the capacity for autonomy) to the extent that therapists have not developed and valued their masculine and feminine self-expression. Until treatments and theories are created and adopted that allow all people to be masculine and feminine, separate and connected, psychotherapy is at least as dangerous as it is helpful. The frame for treatment offered by therapists who are unaware and defensive about genderality, and especially, those who react negatively to expressions of femininity, creates a gendered "superparadox" (Selvini-Palazzoli et al., 1978): "'Its not that you don't do what you should do'; it's that you're not as you should be' (where 'as you should be' obviously remains as vague and undefined as 'what you should do')" (p. 37). Human beings desire autonomy and connection; they are masculine and feminine. Genderality, masculinity and femininity, is a significant and fundamental aspect of any individual's self-experience. The potential for experiencing shame with regard to one's genderality is extremely high. Shame is especially likely to occur in relationships in which the participants have unequal power. Therapy is a particular form of relationship in which the circumstances are likely to evoke shame because one person is unilaterally describing their least effective behaviors, thoughts, and feelings to a more powerful other. The status differential is greatest when the therapist is male because maleness confers additional status. Due to his higher status because of his training and his sex, the therapist has the power to influence the client's self-perceptions and the client's evaluations of them. If the therapist has been trained personally and professionally to value masculinity and to devalue femininity, to locate masculinity in males and femininity in females, to treat women and children in ways that encourage adaptation to traditional sex and gender role expectations, or to unreflectively adopt counter traditional roles based on emerging alternative values, then therapist effectiveness may be seriously compromised because the therapist may behave in punishing, mystifying, binding, and projective ways that disallows the client's process of self-determination and self-discovery in treatment.

Conclusion

Shame is a powerful tool for social control that is especially potent in its effect of validating or invalidating the self. Because shame is experienced in relationship and has the purpose of disconnecting a too intense interaction, shame negatively affects relatedness as well as the sense of self. Continuous and intense evocation of shame can seriously disrupt persons ability to maintain interpersonal attachment, and can force persons into interpersonal silence and into hiding. Evocation of shame is a special instance of hostile dominance, and, as such, coerces an individual's compliance to prescriptions for social behaviors that are determined by a powerful and significant other.

Critical assessments of hostile dominance as a form of social and interpersonal power are currently arising from a variety of disciplines, and there is general agreement that hostile dominance is pathological even though it has been commonly associated with cultural prescriptions for the expression of masculinity. Femininity, described as interpersonal relatedness or tender attachment, has been proposed as a necessary alternative to hostile dominance. However, masculinity can be expressed positively as goal-directed productivity while femininity may be expressed harmfully as grasping and suffocating enmeshment. Healthy power would be exercised in nonhostile mutuality, called "codetermined power." Codetermined power depends fundamentally on mutually constrained freedom and consensus decision-making processes. Each participant is viewed as an agent and as a dependent; each perspective must be taken as information of common concern; action plans must be mutually satisfactory. Codetermined power would be expressed in positive masculine ways and in positive feminine ways.

Two social institutions which have responsibility for training cultural values for appropriate social behaviors are the family and the field of psychotherapy. The representatives of these institutions, parents and therapists, have power because of their being and their training to influence and shape the values and the practices of members of the society. These representatives may be unable to teach appropriate genderality due to their own lack of skills, training, and experience, especially, with regard to healthy expression of femininity. Expression of femininity has been devalued and denigrated in the past. As a result, parents and therapists, particularly fathers and male therapists, may be unable to value and encourage their children's or their clients' expressions of femininity. They may also resist expressions of masculinity by females with whom they associate due to cultural proscriptions. Data indicate that fathers' positive evaluations of genderality, including femininity, are associated with children expressing more diverse aspects of gender. Other data indicate that therapists' inability to value and positively support client change lead to poor therapeutic outcomes. While these studies do not specifically explore therapist influence on client genderality, they do present a possible method for study, and they identify therapist behaviors that are associated with negative outcomes.

The studies of parenting and the studies of psychotherapeutic outcomes suggest that therapists and parents are powerful individuals in relationship to children and clients, and that their interpersonal interactions may evoke shame or pride, emotions which powerfully impact self-valuing, self-expression, and self-exploration. Expressions of power by these high status individuals need to be tempered and supported by careful and continuing self-reflection and personal growth, and by societal commitments to provide adequate resources and education to those who provide emotional care.

Conclusion

This study began with the assertion that there is a connection between the sense of self and voicelessness in the experience of many late 20th century women. A central theme of many current culture tales about women is "voice" (or "voicelessness"), a metaphor which has been used for exploring women's sense of self and women's capacity for self-expression. I have defined "voice" as self-declaration in an interpersonal context that has as a primary goal maintaining interpersonal connection. "Voice" is a metaphor for power, especially personal power, in the social arena. In the past women in the west have experienced themselves as politically and personally powerless when compared to men. The public sphere has been controlled by men politically and economically, and male dominance has been experienced in the home as well.

For several decades, psychologists and philosophers have described women's experience vis-à-vis men's experience. The psychology of women has been dominated by descriptions of women as being just like men, or as being deficient when compared to men. Models of human development proposed by Freud, Erikson, Kohlberg, Piaget, and others have been based on philosophical assumptions that overstate the value of separateness and independence and that negatively value human connection and intimacy. These models described the ego or self as separate, masterful, and independent; they also described the maturational process as developing more separateness over time through winning a power struggle with the mother-other, who resists the child's efforts for self-dominion by willful neglect of the child's reality or by overbearing direction of the child's experience. According to these theorists, men develop more mature cognitive and ethical capacities based on objectivity and individual rights because of their more fully developed separateness due to their sexual difference from the mother. These findings were consistent with more ideologically based assumptions about women and women's roles in society. Theorists assumed that women were less fit in some essential way for professional or public life because they were emotional and interpersonally concerned. Further, assumptions about women's limited mental and moral capacities were based on observations that childcare required physical closeness between mother and child during gestation and lactation as well as emotional availability of the mother to child.

Although early 20th century theories about women were justified by biological "facts," they were heavily influenced by traditions and philosophies that predated scientific inquiry. Prior to the Enlightenment religious leaders and philosophers associated women with evil, evil with lustful sexuality, and lust with unbridled expression of sexual behavior. To a large degree the culture's association of woman with evil was the legacy of gnosticism and stoicism. The common philosophical, psychological, and sociological assumption was that women were intellectually limited due to their biological functions of gestation, parturition, and lactation--an assumption which led to the view that women were more closely connected to nature than men were. Enlightenment notions of progress relied heavily on the premise that the mind and the intellect of man functioned over-against nature and that the purpose of mankind was to overcome or dominate nature through the application of science and technology. Due to the close philosophical association of woman and nature, of nature and finiteness, of finiteness and evil, women were devalued and denigrated by philosophers and rulers in western culture. Philosophical and political ideals suggested that woman, like nature, must be subjugated and ruled by man.

The devaluation and denigration of women has been connected by some thinkers to men's devaluation and denigration of their own feelings of weakness and vulnerability. Although Freud defined woman as "not man" because women had no penises, he could have defined man as "not woman" because men have no wombs. Body and embodied life were strong determinants of social functions, and the reproductive functions, that is the woman's role in carrying, birthing, and feeding the baby from her own body, were central to definitions of femininity. Throughout history femininity and masculinity were closely associated with femaleness and maleness respectively. Women were encouraged to be feminine and not masculine, while men were encouraged to be masculine and not feminine. Among the significant changes wrought by industrialization were changing understandings of women's and men's roles as well as of understandings of masculinity and femininity. Masculinity and femininity came to be associated with nonbiological parental tasks, with spheres of social functioning, and with personality, as well as with biology. With the advent of western industrialization, productive labor was removed from the home. Women stayed at home with young children while men went to the office or the factory. Women and children who had had a role in providing for the ongoing physical welfare of the family did not have an economic role in the family after industrialization occurred. Especially for women and children of the middle and upper economic classes, work that produced tangible goods was replaced by work that produced intangible emotional and intellectual products, such as a pleasant emotional climate in the home or good grades in school. Personal value was still associated with productivity, but women and children were increasingly unproductive. Male children were able to look forward to a time when they would become productive adults, but female children could not. Femaleness and femininity became less and less valuable. In the past femininity had been associated with evil sexuality that robbed men of their strength and will and with physical weakness and vulnerability that negatively affected survival. During the industrialization of western society, femininity and femaleness came to be associated with uselessness and neediness as well.

Freud and his followers defined womanhood as not having a penis and suggested that the woman's sense of self was rooted in her envy of men which arose from not having that important biological apparatus. Horney defined woman as having a vagina and suggested that woman's sense of self was rooted in the awareness of her capacity to bear children. The object relations theorists, who challenged Freudian notions of the child, defined woman as having a breast. Each of these definitions of woman depends heavily on some body part and leads to an understanding of womanhood that is primarily biological. By the middle of the 20th century, theorists had come to define woman as the mother-other against whom the child struggled for independence; the mother was an ever-present reminder to the child of the dependency which he had strived to outgrow. In this case the mother reminded the child of his physical dependency which he had to repudiate in order to take his proper place in adult society.[1] Girls were disadvantaged according to these models of self development because social expectations for girls' and women's roles disallowed the achievement of full separateness that the models declared was full maturity. While these models made woman more than her reproductive biology, they continued to define woman in terms of her relationship with others rather than as a person in her own right. By the 1950s woman was defined psychologically by her social relationship with a child who needed to gain independence from the physical and emotional control of the mother and sociologically by her social relationship with a man from whom she received economic provision.

Twentieth-century definitions of femininity came to include biological, social, parental, and personality characteristics which were devalued and denigrated by the western society in which women lived. Masculinity was defined in terms of self-assertion, independence, and autonomy—human traits which were culturally valued, while femininity was defined in terms of compliance, dependence, and submission—human traits which were culturally devalued and denigrated.

Because of increased opportunities for college level education and increased popular dissemination of academic knowledge through radio, television, and print media, women's self-understandings and self-valuings were increasingly affected by psychological theories of self and self-development. Further, because of increased education women were becoming more intellectually competent at the same time that they were becoming decreasingly challenged by domestic work due to technological and industrial advances that made home care more tedious, less interesting, and less time and energy consuming. Also at the same time, the education of children had become the specialized work of trained experts so that mothers were being encouraged to place their children in school at ever earlier ages. Women needed to feel valued and valuable; they experienced the cultural devaluation and denigration of traditional definitions of womanhood and femininity due to the cultural emphasis on assertion, independence, and productivity. Many women began to look outside the home for meaning, purpose, and value. By the 1970s women were being encouraged to establish themselves as independent, autonomous, and assertive individuals in the public sphere of work in order to gain self-respect and self-esteem, as well as the respect of men. Women were being encouraged by both the popular media and the academy to develop human traits that had been defined in the past as *masculine* and as belonging only to men. Further, they were given ambiguous and ambivalent messages regarding expression of the *feminine*. In the public arena when engaged in functions that had been previously reserved for men only, women were being encouraged to give up traits which had been viewed as *feminine*. While at home, they were responsible for expression of *femininity*, especially in their relations with husbands and children.

The term "gender" was borrowed from grammar to signify the category of human characteristics that were traditionally associated with masculinity and femininity; thus, people could have gender just as words had gender. Researchers and culture commentators distinguished biological features of the human person that determine the sex of an individual from other nonbiological features of the person, including feelings, attitudes, and behaviors, that determine the gender role of the person. Although "gender" was originally used to signify "masculine" and "feminine," it has come to mean "social group membership" and applies to groups that are identified as "men" or "women." This understanding of gender leaves sex and social role seriously confounded. In general speech, "gender" and "sex" are increasingly being used as synonyms. Introduction of the term "gender" was an attempt to clarify and discriminate between biological and nonbiological features of personhood, however, the developing use of the term leaves the biological and nonbiological confounded. I believe this has happened because femininity continues to be devalued and denigrated in western culture in both men and women. Psychological theories and cultural practices of the last 20 years have been attempts to do away with the value-laden concepts of femininity and masculinity, as well as many behaviors that are signified by the concepts. However, this attempt seriously undermines healthy human functioning because femininity is as important and valuable a part of human nature as is masculinity.

More recently, theorizers and researchers—most of them women—have been attempting to address the problem of devaluing and disregarding feminine functioning by studying and describing a variety of "women's ways" of being and doing in the world. They are describing important features of human functioning, all of which are grounded in the recognition of the human need for and positive value of affiliation and interpersonal connection. However, these new theories are in danger of asserting in reverse the argument of Freud and others that to be different in function is to be different in value, because of the implicit value given to connection versus separateness and because of the explicit description that connection is woman's, and not man's, way. The explicit and implicit gender confusion that exists is due to the use of a definition of "gender" that confounds biology and social category, "male" social group and "female" social group. One way out of this confounded understanding that will allow men and women to function in connected and separate ways is to reserve the term "gender" to signify only aspects of human functioning that are expressions of personality, rather than biology, social sphere, or parental role.[2] Men (fundamentally a biological category that is based on identifying characteristics that are biosexual) may nurture and connect as well as assert and separate, and women (also a biosexual category) may separate and assert as well as connect and nurture. Although emphasizing the positive value of women's ways helps to correct the imbalance caused by overvaluing autonomy and separateness, this approach implicitly devalues and denigrates maleness by confusing maleness with masculinity and femaleness with femininity. I suggested the term "genderality" as a category of personality expression to signify those feelings, attitudes, and behaviors that are associated with masculinity and femininity, but that are nonbiologically determined.

Masculine assertiveness and separateness have been overvalued while feminine receptivity and connectedness have been undervalued or negatively valued. The valuation of these human gender traits and the manner in which the valuation is communicated create powerful social prescriptions and proscriptions for gendered self-expression. Human beings come to know themselves in some fundamental way as sexed human beings—that is, as male or female. Biology is reality, though it is not destiny. Historically, maleness has been valued over femaleness. In addition, social behaviors, feelings, and ideas that have been identified with men and the masculine have been valued over social behaviors, feelings, and ideas that have been identified with women and the feminine. However, many of these characteristics are not sexed male or female; they are not determined by biological factors. Rather, they are learned through social interaction and they are trained through the use of punishing or rewarding responses made by significant others in the social environments of individuals. Because genderality is conflated with sexuality and then treated in devaluing ways, those persons who "inappropriately" exhibit gendered self-expression are punished, humiliated, and belittled. Prescriptions for appropriate and proscriptions of inappropriate gendered self-expression create reinforcing environments that evoke shame.

Shame is an affective response to assaults from the interpersonal environment that fundamentally reject the person and undermine the basic sense of self. It is extremely common for children to be shamed for behaving in gendered inappropriate (as designated by the social environment) ways. Boys have commonly been shamed for behaving in feminine ways: a practice which leads to reactive hypermasculine self-expression in boys as well as to reactive rejection by boys of female figures and any close association with them. Girls and women have also faced increasing social pressure to reject their femininity. At the same time, boys and men continue to project femininity onto and into females, making women and girls solely responsible for the expression of femininity in interpersonal relations and for its concomitant shame. It may be especially likely for boys to be shamed by fathers and mothers, by teachers and coaches, and by male peers for behaving in feminine ways. This particular susceptibility in males to the evocation of shame for expressing feminine features of the self may be related to a variety of experiences related to maleness and to males' process of socialization.

There is mounting evidence that males suffer from a variety of genetic, hormonal, and neurological syndromes that make them constitutionally weaker and more prone to illness and neurological and cognitive dysfunction than females. At the same time that they are more at risk for the development of dysfunction, they are trained in a social environment that demands behavior and attitudes which exacerbate the risk factors and negatively impact the dysfunctions. Because they are more likely to experience dysfunctions that increase physical and emotional dependency on caregivers while being trained to eschew need and dependency, male human beings may become frustrated, afraid, and lonely. Further, they may experience repeated exposure to shame and to shaming responses from significant others because they are unable to perform in the masculine ways that are prescribed by their social milieu. The boy is trapped in a negative feedback loop that requires that he behave in a way that he cannot and is punished for both his attempts and his failures. Rather than receiving help and encouragement from his social environment, he is punished, belittled, and humiliated for his honest self-expressions as well as his attempts to live up to the expectations of independence that are beyond his ability. Although the young male child may have specific physiological vulnerabilities that need special attention, one must not assume that he is destined by his biology to misbehavior, aggression, and other asocial or antisocial behavior; repeated experiences of failure and shame create rage, hostility, and a desire for revenge. In attempts to ward off shame and humiliation, the male attacks the female. Attacks may be physical, or they may be emotional and/or psychological. More often than not caregivers are female in western culture; the young child experiences the female caregiver as strong and powerful. Boy children may experience female caregivers as powerful, but withholding or abusive of that power. Boys may want to snatch that feminine power, or they may want to spoil that power. At the same time they want to minimize that power. A variety of attacking methods may serve the boy in his attempts to deal with feminine power. When the social environment is continually reinforcing of the double bind of denying real weakness while requiring nonexistent or limited strength in boys' self-experience, boys may grow into men who hate and envy women. The sense of deprivation and rage over the deprivation may be intensified in the many boys who have no positive male caregivers to train the boys into roles, rights, and responsibilities of male adulthood. In relationships with men, women may experience emotional and psychological pressure to become the feminine for themselves and for the man. Because femininity is devalued and denigrated—that is, shamed—by western culture practices, women will feel ashamed of their femininity. Because femininity is associated with weakness and vulnerability and with shame, especially for and by men, women will be *punished* for being the weakness that is the despised aspect of men's own personality. Women may experience men's femininity and the shame related to it through a variety of psychological mechanisms that function in social systems as means for maintaining relationship in stable, but unhealthy, homeostasis. *Mystification* serves to keep one member of an interpersonal system confused about the real nature of the communication between the members in an attempt to avoid direct experience of conflict. With relation to gender, mystification would serve to keep the woman unaware of the man's need for her to be the feminine one in order to avoid his awareness of his femininity and the conflict that he feels in relation to his femininity. The *double bind* is a special form of mystification that leaves the woman who remains in the communication system with no alternative action than the one prescribed by the mystifying message which simultaneously demands and disallows a given behavior. For example, the message "women cannot be angry" creates a paradox for the woman who allows the message sender to be in control of the definition of *woman* and of the rule of womanly conduct: If she is angry, she is not a woman; if she is a woman, she is not angry. In either case the woman so defined may not be what she is. *Projective identification* is another mechanism for getting rid of forbidden femininity: A man cannot tolerate consciously experiencing his own femininity, so he unconsciously projects it into the woman with whom he has the relationship. When she receives his femininity as if it is her own, she begins to think, feel, and act his thoughts, feelings, and actions. If he responds to "her" with the rage and rejection that he feels against his own femininity, then she experiences his self-rejection as a rejection of her. He has not had to take responsibility for his own feminine strivings nor for his contempt for them. The woman has become the victim and scapegoat of his self-directed primitive superego process, and he remains unscathed by his own self-hatred. Finally, shame of femininity may be, and has been, induced in women by punishment. Quite simply women are punished for exhibiting feminine thoughts, feelings, and behaviors, and they learn to avoid the self-expressions associated with the consequent punishment.

Shaming is a powerful form of interpersonal communication. Belittling, humiliating, and attacking behavior are extremely threatening to a person's physical and psychological integrity. Individuals will make every attempt to physically or psychically escape the shaming person and/or environment. Fierce aggression and dominance are forms of power that rely on bullying and belittling behavior and have been associated with cultural definitions of masculinity. More subtle belittling may be done by women (particularly mothers) who attempt to coerce others to behave as the women choose. In both cases power, or social influence, has been exerted in an attempt to obtain a desired goal without regard to the needs and desires of the other. Power may be expressed directly as a command which must be obeyed, or it may be expressed as provoking behavior which passively elicits the desired behavior from the other without a direct command. Shame may be especially provocative, as opposed to commanding, because it calls attention to what the person is not rather than to what the person is. When one has been shamed, a person's initial response will be to attempt to hide from the displeased other. The hiding will be followed by attempts to become what the other wanted, even if the other has not stated what that desire is. However, another common feature of the shame reaction is bypassed or expressed anger at the shaming other who has so much power over the one shamed. It seems logical and likely that genderality would be especially susceptible to shaming and rage reactions because it is experienced as a fundamental part of a person's nature. It also seems logical and likely that if boys are especially prone to weakness and failure in the face of significant adults' expectations that they would make every attempt to avoid or get rid of the shameful and shaming features of their personalities that are associated with the adults' displeasure. If women are susceptible to receiving the shameful features of personality because of their social training in interpersonal connection and in expecting men to be not feminine, then they will be more likely to carry femininity and shame for that femininity in themselves. If one feature of shame is hiding and another feature of shame is rage then it is likely that women will experience their own and men's femininity, shame over that femininity, rage at being shamed, and silence in attempts to hide from the shaming other. Further, women will attempt to remain silent so as not to displease the other either with unacceptable anger or unacceptable femininity. It is not surprising that women are voiceless with regard to the expression of femininity in western culture. Silence keeps the feminine from being expressed, and it keeps the shameful feminine self-expression out of danger of being attacked. When women manage femininity and shame over femininity for both men and women, men can pretend that they have no femininity of which to be ashamed. Increasingly, women have attempted a solution similar to men's of the dilemma of genderality: Women have attempted to become more autonomous and separate in order to succeed in the public sphere and to repudiate their relational needs and desires. Other women have attempted assertions of the positive value of women's ways without attending to the possibilities of reverse sexism, sex bias, and distortion inherent in such formulations. "Masculine" and "feminine" continue to be commonly used terms when references are made to gendered self-expressions. The continued use of these terms in the discipline of psychology without making careful definitions of them risks continuing confusion of biologically determined and nonbiological aspects of human functioning. However, to discontinue the use of difficult terms that are in the everyday vocabulary of ordinary people risks being a discipline that cannot communicate with those it seeks to understand and serve. I would encourage taking the risk of using common terms in carefully defined ways so that psychologists can study the psychological experiences that ordinary people are referring to when they use the terms. Psychologists must also be careful to understand and to evaluate the value placed on the functions signified by the terms. In order for psychologists to study and to treat well and wisely, they must attend to the power of shame and social behaviors which evoke shame when dealing with sexuality and genderality. Men and women are ashamed of femininity; they are sensitive to the value that is assigned to expressions of femininity by significant others in their social environment. Men may be especially likely to avoid feminine self-expression or to project their femininity on significant women. As a result women may have more responsibility for feminine self-expression and for feelings of its concomitant shame in cross-sexed communication systems. Therapists who work with men, women, and families must become acutely aware of social definitions of masculinity and femininity, of the valuation assigned to them, and of the potential for shame associated with the expression of them. Only with that acute awareness and sensibility will therapists and teachers be able to de-shame gender and gender relations.

Developmental theory is being reoriented. Beyond descriptions of men's ways and beyond descriptions of women's ways, there is beginning to emerge a description of a human way of development that accounts for the need for separateness and the need for connection, the need for autonomy and relationship, the need for independence and intimacy. If these theories that describe both aspects of human experience continue to gain academic and research support, it may soon be possible to drop the problematic concept of gender. In the meantime, use of the terms "masculine" and "feminine," as expressions of human personality, can be useful because these terms are commonly used and have commonly understood meanings that signify important aspects of human experience. However, use of the terms "feminine" and "masculine" must be accompanied by a sensitivity to the probability that use of these labels will elicit feelings of shame. Because femininity has long been devalued and denigrated in western culture, and because femaleness is a closely associated concept that has also been devalued in western culture, identifying feminine thoughts, feelings, and behaviors will like induce a shame response. In therapy, the shame must be accepted, understood, and dismantled. In theory formation and experimental testing the shame reaction must be explored and understood.

As has been suggested throughout this study, the Structural Analysis of Social Behavior may provide an extremely helpful method for exploring genderality and its relationship with shame in both therapy and research. It may be fruitful to apply the SASB model to identify gendered self-expression, to explore the complementary and oppositional natures of masculinity and femininity, to investigate the complexity of gendered self-expression, and to understand the mechanisms of the evocation of shame in gendered self-expression. Further, it may be useful in undertaking investigations of power and interpersonal influence and it may further psychological understanding of abusive versus nonabusive expressions of power.

Epilogue.
Sustenance Culture Tales

We began this study with a reflection on current culture tales which appear to have cultural and personal significance, especially for women. I will close with a reflection on current culture tales of boys' search for sustenance. If women have been portrayed as voiceless; boys are being portrayed as hungry for and isolated from social connection. The method of this analysis is somewhat different from the earlier analysis of women's tales; that analysis began with an intuitive awareness of the organizing theme of voicelessness. The analysis of the boys' tales is vitally influenced by the elaboration of the material in this study and by accepting the products of the study to freshly influence the experience of the stories.

The current culture tales are *Aladdin* (Musker & Clements, 1993), *The Lion King* (Hahn, Allers, & Minkoff, 1994), *Jungle Book* (Feldman & Summers, 1995) and *Home Alone* (Hughes & Columbus, 1990). These stories share several features: fatherless and motherless boys, left to raise themselves; an encounter with evil others who are like themselves in their maleness; dependence on their own wits and skill for survival, with dubious support from similar others (except in *Home Alone* in which the upper class white boy is truly alone); the arrival of seemingly magical help (except in *Home Alone)*; the engagement of a helpful and competent female other (except in *Home Alone)*; the vanquishing of an evil other; and the establishment of a social bond with a community of character.

These tales seem to reflect mythologically the circumstances which are described in the research of Stevens and Gardner (1994). *Home Alone* is, perhaps, the most disturbing tale, and best fits the description of Stevens and Gardner. The parents are self-absorbed and materialistic; They are harsh with and neglectful of their son. When he is left home alone, he valiantly takes up the adult work left to him and survives an evil onslaught that is simply fantastic. While the survival and its technique of achievement are heroic, they are vacuous feats: The protection of a house, empty of people and full of things, that is accomplished only through the grossest of human and material destruction.

The other tales, coming as they do from earlier eras but recently retold, may offer a hope that is not felt in the portrayal of a more immediate emotional ethos. In *Aladdin*, *The Lion King*, and *The Jungle Book* there are reliable but flawed adult figures. The initial loss of the child is the result of significant upheaval in the environment, rather than of parental narcissism. The well-being of a community is being protected, rather than a house full of goods. The denouement of the tales involve the establishment of family and the restoration of community, rather than the salvaging of the family home and the mother's self-respect. Let us hope that *Aladdin*, *The Lion King*, and *The Jungle Book* reveal for us what lies ahead, and that *Home Alone* is merely a klaxon sounding to warn the culture of the danger that its sons are facing in a world that is run by "empty selves" brandishing "identity politics" in order to hide from unfulfilled infantile need.

Notes

Introduction. Women and Voicelessness

[1] Chapter 4 will identify and elaborate some salient features of the silencing of women's voices.

[2] See Eurich-Rascoe (1990a, 1990b) for a treatment of the psychological implications of two of these current culture tales.

A number of psychologists from a variety of subdisciplines discuss the importance of story and narrative in gaining understanding of persons and their experience of their own humanity, as well as the importance of narrative to the practice of psychotherapy and to the field of psychology. See Howard, 1991; Josselson and Lieblich, 1993; Lee, 1993; McAdams, 1993; McFague, 1982; Schafer, 1992; Van Leeuwen, 1984; Vitz, 1990.

[3] Berger and Luckman (1967) suggest that "reality" and "knowledge" of that reality are "socially constructed." They refer to Mannheim (1936), who state that society determines "not only the appearance but also the content of human ideation" (p. 9) and that epistemology always has a particular point of view. Thus, any object of thought is always perceived and apperceived from a particular location that can lead to idealizing that view of the object. In order to solve this problem of over-reliance on a paerticular viewpoint, Mannheim stated that the accumulation of a variety of perspectives would clarify the object of thought. In the construction of social reality, Mannheim believed, that individual social groups have difficulty "transcend[ing] their own narrow postion[s]" (p. 10) and taht "historicism," recognition "that no historical situation could be understood except in its own terms" (p. 7) provides the needed transcendance. According to these formulations, all knowers are "constructive," and the apperception that males are "objective" is itself a social construction of reality. See Chapter 2 for further discussion of the social construction of gender.

For and excellent, but brief, discussion of "historiscism" in psychology, the reader is referred to G. W. Stocking (1965), On the limits of 'presentism' and 'historicism' in the historiography of the behavioral sciences. An entirely different definition of historicism, focusing on the failure to distinguish between scientific prediciton and historical prophecy, is offered by the philosopher of science Karl Pooper (1957), in *The Poverty of Historicism*.

[4] Visual metaphors long dominated philosophy and philosophical psychology. Aristotle suggested that the mind was a "tabula rasa," a "blank slate," upon which experience writes—the metaphor Locke used to launch modern empiricism. Visual metaphors are also indicated by Aristotle's positing of the faculty of imagination (the image-forming capacity) which was said to be a prerequisite of thinking; Aquinas further systematized this psychological concept. The ability to "look within," or observe one's own mental processes, was essential to Titchenerian introspection. The existence of these mental images was challenged in several ways after the launching of the new, experimental psychology. Galton was interested in mental images and set about studying them empirically. His instructions to his subjects assumed that they thought in images, and he was surprised to find that many of them denied having any imagery (Watson, 1978). David Murray (1983) says of J. B. Watson: "As for imagery, he felt that all cases of so-called visual imagery could be analyzed into cases of verbalization. Since this conflicts with the introspective experience of many persons, it has been suggested that Watson himself lacked visual imagery" (pp. 277–78).

[5] The term "process" is meant in its ordinary sense as any series of operations leading to a goal, rather than in the technical sense in which it is used in cognitive psychology.

[6] Definitions are from *Merriam-Webster's Collegiate Dictionary*, 1993.

[7] Notice the assumption in this discussion of a tripartite model of human personality. This model is first described by Kant and was developed by Ward (1886). The tripartite personality is based on "Kant's distinction between cognition, affection, and conation" (Flugel, 1933, p. 151). The classic exposition of this is James Ward's article on "Psychology" in the *Encyclopaedia Britannica* in 1886.

[8] See Baumrind (1992) for further critique of Kohlberg; she rejects a definition of moral maturity that "exclude[s] the practical consequences for the self" as "inhumane and unrealizable" (p. 265).

[9] The very fact that there is a special word to indicate the feminine in the male may indicate the special relationship that the male has to his own

"femininity." That word is "effeminate," and it is not simply a synonym for feminine. It carries a somewhat derogatory connotation which suggests that when a man "is effeminate" he is misbehaving or has been malformed in some way; one wonders if he has been "emasculated." There are no equivalent words to apply to females. More will be said about this in Chapter 4.

[10]This is not a dilemma for women only; men, too, have no voice for the expression of certain experiences, particularly of their femininity. This will be taken up in Chapter 4.

[11]The contradiction here is like those that underlie theories relating to paradoxical communication and the logical structure of the double bind, situations which lead to symptoms because what is mere nonsense at the semantic level becomes a behavioral impasse at the pragmatic level. In fact, the contradiction might be understood as a situation in which symmetrical and complementary definitions of a relationship are being offered simultaneously. Such situations are discussed in Watzlawick, Beavin, & Jackson (1967) in the section (6.4) on pragmatic paradoxes. This discussion relies heavily on the theory of logical types, and a woman's confusion in these situations can be reduced if she gains awareness of the conflation of logical types.

[12]Voicelessness (as well as loss of thoughts, the mental voice) and hiding are hallmarks of the shame reaction. The connection between shame and voice will be discussed further in Chapter 4.

Chapter 1. Identity and Voice

[1]This emphasis influences perceptions of the health and well-being of Asians and other two-thirds world peoples as well as that of women. (See Kobayashi, 1989)

[2]The concept of a "self-in-relation" was alluded to by Gilligan (1982) and developed by the psychologists at the Stone Center for Developmental Services and Studies at Wellesley College. Basically, "self-in-relation" is a concept that recognizes that interpersonal relationship is fundamental to women's experiential and developmental sense of who they are. See the section, Self-in-Relationship, in this chapter.

[3]A computerized search using PsychLit (American Psychological Association) to survey the literature on the psychology of women from 1974 to 1988 revealed thousands of articles about women and autonomy and the development of more autonomy, and none on relatedness, affiliation, or connection. Key words searched were: woman, women, female, sex, gender, autonomy, relatedness, affiliation, connection.

⁴See Chapter 4 for a more complete discussion of shame.

⁵See Josselson (1992) for an elaboration of the developmental process of attachment.

⁶See C. G. Jung (1931, 1933/1971), Ellenberger (1970) for further discussion of Jung's theory.

⁷For further reflection on discourse between dominant and underclass social groups see Butler (1990) and Steele (1989, 1990).

⁸This description of the family is similar to the understanding of Minuchin and Fishman (1981). They adopt Koestler's (1979) term **holon** to designate the bonded separateness of the various units that make up the part-wholes of any group. "Each whole contains the part, and each part also contains the 'program' that the whole imposes" (p. 13).

⁹A very different reconstruction of Erikson's stage theory is presented by Schreck (1991), who suggests that the stages and products of Industry, Identity, Intimacy, and Integrity exist in mutually interacting relationships with one another that may be modeled as a pyramid with each stage at one of each of the four corners of the pyramid. With this model he is attempting to account for observed experience which he believes has been neglected in other work: (a) The clearer recognition and description of "relational life tasks" in Erikson's theory, and (b) the incorporation of spirituality in Erikson's theory. I am impressed with this psychospiritual model of social development, and I think that This model would be even stronger and more useful if Schreck had included the stage of Generativity as one of the four corners of the pyramid and placed Integrity at its center.

¹⁰Avoidance of eye contact is a marker event in the shame response. See Chapter 4.

¹¹See Blatt and Blass (1990) for more descriptions of these views of human nature.

¹²See Tabin (1994) for further discussion of this issue.

¹³As we shall see in Chapter 4, affect language is a particularly potent device in the communication of shame.

¹⁴Luepnitz (1988) suggests that those who are researching women's and men's differences may be inadvertently contributing to this misconstrual by overstating what difference exists. Spelman (1988) and Bregman and Thiermann (1995) also critique the gender difference paradigms.

Chapter 2. Gender: Feminine and Maculine Defined

[1] Feminist scholars disagree on the "essential" nature of sex and gender. According to Judith Butler (1990), a feminist historian, much of progressive feminist thought makes both explicit and implicit assumptions that "gender" and "sex" are true and natural categories which have "essential" meaning apart from the culture that creates and defines the identities and relationships which the terms signify. She criticizes feminist discourse for assuming that its feminist-defined "woman" is any more real, more essential than the "woman" of masculinist thought. She states, "The feminist 'we' is always and only a phantasmatic construction" (p. 142). In this study, I make the point, contrary to Butler's, that body is real and, therefore, that "sex," "male," and "female" signify some embodied reality. I agree with Butler's conclusion that the body is not "essential," but what I mean by that is that biology is not destiny. Butler rejects embodiment because she believes that political discourse on embodiment has been used to subjugate women and homosexuals; her rejection of body suggests that she may believe that biology is destiny. I believe that sex and gender differences have been used as instruments of subjugation; however, embodiment does not necessarily determine social or political life. I believe that to reject the reality of physicality leads to far greater problems than it solves.

[2] See Berger and Luckmann (1967) and footnote 4 in the Introduction for a discussion of social construction.

[3] See MMPI (Hathaway & McKinley, 1967); MMPI-2 (Hathaway & McKinley, 1989); CPI (Gough, 1957); and Bem, 1974.

[4] The term "androgyny" derives from Greek mythology and its tale of the god, Androgynos, the son of Aphrodite and Hermes, who had physical aspects of both the male and the female. There are many stories of Primordial unity between the masculine and the feminine, including the biblical narrative of creation that states, "in the image of God [God] created them, male and female [God] created them" (Genesis 1:26; emphasis added). Further, the word is formed by joining two Greek words—*andros*, meaning man; and *gyn*, meaning woman—thus, the man-woman (see Singer, 1976). For other discussion of androgyny see in Chapters 3, 5 and 6.

[5] This understanding of the orthogonality of masculine and feminine has not been incorporated into the most recent revision of the MMPI-2. This is a serious limitation of the usefulness of Scale 5 of the test; and, perhaps, passivity and aggression would be more accurate descriptors for this scale. There is no evidence that the gender-role literature was considered in the redesign of the instrument (Butcher, personal communication, September 27, 1991). Gender sensitivity and accurate definitions of gender are

imperative in providing culture-fair testing. Accurate assessment of persons' psychological states is dependent on appropriate operational definitions and accurate application of psychological research. Further consideration of personality tests is beyond the scope of this paper.

[6]Several recent studies review the literature on sex differences; I will summarize three. Maccoby's (1990) summary states that "behavioral differentiation between the sexes is minimal when children are observed or tested individually. Sex differences emerge in social situations, and their nature varies with the gender composition of the dyads and groups" (p. 513) In another review of the literature, Jacklin (1989) argues that the data suggest "that gender is not an important variable in the measure of intellectual abilities" (p. 131); that measures of some biological variables show evidence of gender differences but "their importance in children's behavioral development is not yet known" (p. 131) and that the causal relationship between biological variables and behavioral outcomes is extremely difficult to determine; and that the area of socialization research has yielded "[m]any empirical studies [which] both support and refute current theoretical positions [on sex differences]. ... Gender roles and division of labor may play a strong role in causing gender differences." Riger (1992) reviews and critiques feminist methods in the practice of psychology and suggests that there appear to be few true sex differences between women and men, and that most of the observed differences between men and women are "constituted by the myriad ways in which we 'do' rather than 'have' gender" (p. 737).

In contrast to Maccoby (1990), Jacklin (1989) and Riger (1992), Moir and Jessel (1991) summarily present an interpretation of the biological data from psychoneurological research of the last two decades, concluding that most, if not all, socially expressed sex differences are due to biological differences between males' and females' genetic, hormonal, and neurological natures and that the differences are relatively unchangeable, especially for men whose brains are irreversibly altered during gestation by constant exposure to high levels of testosterone. At the time of its release their controversial argument received wide media coverage, probably because the American public is eager for help in simplifying relationships between men and women. However, the credibility of their presentation is severely hampered by the polemical antifeminist and antimale tone of their social commentary.

(Notice in this discussion the various uses of "gender" and "sex." Do the uses of the two words truly distinguish between the two different concepts as hoped? I don't think so: "gender"="sex"="man" or "woman"="male" or "female.")

[7]I believe that there are two underlying assumptions affecting current uses of the word "gender": (a) a desire to reflect the belief that primary and secondary biological sexual characteristics have minimal impact on social

behavior, and (b) a recognition that the term "sex" is often used to signify the expression of genital sexual behavior rather than to refer to the biological nature of persons. The use of "gender" to refer to "men and women as social groups" (*APA Manual*, p. 47) is an attempt to de-emphasize the role of the body and its parts in determining personhood.

[8]Long before the advent of sex-role research, Jungian depth psychologists were defining "feminine" and "masculine" according to this psychological understanding of gender (without using the term "gender") as a socially defined cluster of traits that tended to be expressed differentially, but not exclusively, depending on the respective femaleness or maleness of the individual. C. G. Jung (1931) believed that the incorporation of behaviors, feelings and attitudes of the opposite sex (i.e., "contrasexual" traits) was essential to the full maturity and human capacity of the individual. See Chapters 1 and 3.

[9]Of particular interest in this study is how this distinction will help us to understand what sexed and/or gendered experience that is represented by "voice" is silenced and why.

[10]These traits have also been associated with the "soul," as opposed to the "spirit" which has traditionally been associated with maleness and masculinity. Jung borrowed the Latin term *anima* (Eng., "soul") to designate the inner, "feminine," spiritually-oriented aspect of the male. He believed that the mid-life project of the male is to come into a conscious relationship to this aspect of his personality. During earlier stages of development, the male pulls away from the primary outer figure who represents the "feminine" to him (i.e., the mother, and represses and suppresses attitudes, feelings, and behaviors that he identifies with her). According to Jung, these feminine traits need to be restored to consciousness in order for spiritual and mental health and wholeness to occur.

Further, Jung and his successors in depth psychology have critiqued western culture for its loss of soul. They suggest that western culture has overemphasized the importance of spirit. The mental life and its domination of the material world. They suggest that a restoration of a positive valuing the feminine and the soul by the culture is imperative (Hillman, 1975, 1979, 1985). For a discussion of soul and its place in psychology see Vande Kemp, 1982a, 1982b, 1983.

[11]These traits have been associated with "spirit" (*pneuma*) by C. G. Jung (1933/1971), E. Jung (1972), Harding (1970), Hillman (1985), and Singer (1972, 1976).

[12]Herein may lie one source for the taboo against homosexual behavior: persons of a particular sex should not engage in the sex- or gender-identity behaviors of the opposite sex.

[13] The Levitical prohibitions regarding uncleanness referred to seminal fluids as well as to menses. The laws of Leviticus have been applied and misapplied inconsistently and variously by Christians. See Ranke-Heinemann (1990) for a thorough treatment of these issues.

[14] See Ranke-Heinemann (1990) for a thorough treatment of this issue.

[15] For a more thorough description of the model's development and of its historical antecedents see Benjamin, 1974, 1993.

[16] Independent of Sullivan, others have developed similar understandings of the primacy of the need for relationship. See object relations theories Mahler (1975), Winnicott (1963, 1971); the infant development research of Stern (1985); the intersubjectivity theory of Stolorow and Atwood (1992) and Stolorow, Brandchaft, and Atwood, 1987; the personalism of MacMurray (1961) or Guntrip (1957); symbolic interactionism of Mead (1964); and the self psychology of Kernberg (1984) and Kohut (1971).

[17] Details on coding procedures appear in Benjamin et al. (1986).

[18] The full version of the SASB Model appears in "Structural analysis of differentiation failure," L. S. Benjamin 1979, *Psychiatry, 42*, 1–23.

[19] This equation may provide another source for taboos on homosexual practice.

[20] As Jacklin (1989) commented, "We rarely wonder whether blue-eyed and brown-eyed or short and tall children differ from one another in intellectual abilities or personality" (p. 127) as we do so often wonder about the effects of maleness and femaleness. Eye color might seem trivial but, as Morrison (1970) points out in the novel *The Bluest Eye*, to an African-American woman eye color can be a source of envy and shame. To a young woman who has learned that *blue* eyes are the only "beautiful" eyes haveing brown eyes becomes a source of shame, a cause for self-rejection. When what she cannot be or become is the measure of her goodness, she can never discover or appreciate the goodness which is already hers.

[21] Projective identification (Ogden, 1982) occurs in the following way:
"First, there is an unconscious fantasy of projecting a part of oneself into another person and of that part taking over the person from within. Then, there is a pressure exerted through the interpersonal interaction such that the recipient of the projection experiences pressure to think, feel, and behave in a manner congruent with the projection. Finally, after being 'psycho-

logically processed' by the recipient, the projected feelings are reinternalized by the projector" (p. 12).

The intersubjective transaction creates, negates and preserves aspects of the projector's and of the receiver's separate subjectivities while creating a third subjectivity in which "each is limited and enriched; each is stifled and vitalized [in the experience of a shared 'I-ness'] through which thoughts might be thoughts, feelings might be felt, sensations might be experienced, which to that point had existed only as potential experiences for each of the individuals participating in this psychological-interpersonal process" (Ogden, 1994). See Chapter 4 for further discussion of gender and projective identification.

[22]See Fine-Thomas (1993) for a treatment of "gender guilt" a phrase referring to the felt experience of some individuals that they are ontologically defective because they are the sex that they are rather than the sex that they are not, or that they are sexed at all.

[23]This raises interesting religious questions. A fuller understanding of the incarnation might view it as God's attempt, through the personality and methods of Jesus, to redeem and to reestablish the positive value of the feminine, since Jesus was (though male and masculine) gentle, tender, interested in children and women, passive, receptive, caring, nurturing, and so forth. Psychologically speaking, a positive experience of the incarnation at the time of conversion to faith may serve as a reparative instance of projective identification. However, further consideration of this interesting theological point is beyond the scope of this study.

Chapter 3. A Brief History of Sex and Gender

[1]Thomas Aquinas viewed women as the "occasion of sin" because women were the active subjects who tempted spiritual men into "evil" (unspiritual) carnal indulgence. Aquinas boasted of the fact that he could not remain in the same room with a woman (Ranke-Heinemann, 1990). He experienced what today would probably be diagnosed as panic attacks.

[2]A similar phenomenon swept through Europe during the Dark Ages. Sprenger & Kraemer (1487/1971), two Dominican monks, wrote *Malleus Maleficarum*, a handbook on how to identify, catch, and kill witches. Conservative estimates suggests that thousands of women, many of whom were healers and midwives, were executed in this way (Ranke-Heinemann, 1990).

[3]n the late 19th century Nietzsche (1844–1900) espoused nihilism, a related philosophy closely related to gnosticism, that denies the existence of any basis for knowledge or truth. Nietzsche believed that the Superman— an idealized, superior, dominating man—is the goal of the evolutionary

struggle for survival; attainment of absolute power and its use for Man's domination of the material world is the role of the Superman (Durant, 1926; "Nietzsche" and "nihilism," *Webster's New World College Dictionary*, 1964).

[4] This line of reasoning is contrary to Freud's observations and conceptualizations. See Freud and the Freudians below. It also contradicts the Augustinian view of woman as temptress. Thus, in the view through history, woman is regarded as either oversexed or neutered (the prostitute or the Madonna), but never "normally sexed" as are men (allegedly).

[5] Shame is the logical counterpart to envy, and the opposite of pride. Gender and shame will be discussed in Chapter 4.

[6] It seems odd that so many competent, achieving women of this generation who accomplished much in distinguished public careers came to such limited conclusions about women in general while living in contradiction to their own theories. See also the discussion by Mead (1949) later in this chapter.

[7] See *Bem and Androgyny* later in this chapter. Also, see *Sex and Gender* in Chapter 1.

[8] It is curious that Mead did not live by this rule herself. She had an active, successful career and a difficult marriage. According to her daughter, Mead was an intent problem-solver and organizer throughout her life, while her husband was inclined to "seek understanding [rather than change] . . . and had a kind of abhorrence for the effort to solve problems" (Bateson, 1984, p. 176). Her attitude toward life, as described by her daughter, has a decidedly masculine quality. Bateson (1984) also describes her mother as having "sustained a network of relations around herself" (p. 16) that suggests a capacity for feminine relatedness as well.

[9] Perhaps, Mead's reaction is evidence of a lasting effect of Romanticism, which was literary, artistic, and philosophical movement (late 18th and early 19th centuries) that emphasized the imagination and the emotions, and placed a positive value on the organic. Further, the movement exalted the primitive and common man. Writers whose work typifies the movement are Coleridge, Shelley, and Wordsworth ("Romanticism," in *Merriam-Webster's Collegiate Dictionary*, 1993; Norberg, personal communication, April 16, 1995). In the history of philosophical and cultural movements, there seems to be a continuing dialectic expressed between (a) nature, body, emotionality and (b) technology, spirit, rationality.

[10]See Chapter 2 and its discussion of the confounded variables in current definitions of gender.

[11]That rejection and repudiation of the mother is a "must" in the boy's experience is an a priori assumption that belies value-laden assumptions about the mother-son relationship. Chodorow shares this assumption with Bly (1990) and Johnson (1990). Lerman (1986) also critiques Chodorow. By adopting psychoanalytic assumptions uncritically Chodorow has objectified and vilified the mother in a wholly unacceptable way (Swigart, 1991).

[12]Compare this process of identity formation to the process described by Freud for women as presented earlier in this chapter; both are identities based on negation of an external other rather than positive assertions of self-experience. Are children really so empty and void?

[13]See Dinnerstein (1976) for further discussion of these issues.

[14]This process of assigning value will be taken up in more detail in Chapter 4.

[15]Gray describes a number of behavioral and attitudinal sex differences that could be summarized as follows: men solve problems; women feel in relationships. His implication is that behaving in a cross-sexed way is inappropriate, which could induce shame. In general, he locates the "masculine" in males and the "feminine" in females and suggests that the two groups are species alien to each other. He gives similar behaviors different labels depending on the sex of the actor, a practice which can only lead to confusion about sex differences. He states that differences between men and women are "natural," yet his goal is to teach couples to understand and behave in new (unnatural and alien?) ways.

[16]This is not historically accurate, as women have cared for each other in the harems of polygamy in the ancient world, in the multigenerational extended family of preindustrial and early industrial societies, in the servant households of the bourgeoisie, and in the nuclear family neighborhood groups of middle 20th-century western societies. Men have not provided "care," they have provided economic support. This misrepresentation may be an instance of describing a wish as if it were a fact. It is only very recently, and only in the west, that companionship in marriage has become a valued goal (See Haffner, 1986; Hymowitz & Weissman, 1978; Kimmel, 1987).

[17]The need for these functions is based on assumptions and value judgments about the mother which are negative and hostile, and have not been empirically determined. Further they rest on assumptions that the

father is absent prior to this period of development (see Biller, 1969; Chodorow, 1978; Dinnerstein, 1976; Hetherington & Deur, 1971; Johnson, M., 1986; Phares, 1992; Stevens & Gardner, 1994; Swigart, 1991).

Chapter 4. Shame and Femininity

[1] The rest of her treatment of perversions uses male perversions as a model by which she can find and describe the "female perversions."

[2] See Chapter 3 for a description of Chodorow's argument.

[3] In the following discussion, Stevens and Gardner appear to hold mothers responsible for much of what goes wrong for boys. While I understand that their psychodynamic orientation necessarily points in the mother's direction, I would encourage more careful and reflective testing of this hypothesis. I am uncomfortable with assigning mothers so much power and responsibilities. The mother must become a subject in the eyes of psychological researchers and theorizers as well as being construed as the infants' object-other. See Swigart (1991) for a further treatment of this position.

[4] Angyal's (1941) term "homonomy" implies "the integration of the individual into the social group, the assimilation of [the group] culture, of its written and unwritten codes" (pp. 167–207).

[5] See also Knoppers (1993) which cites the work of the Office for Sex Equity in Education (1989) which reports school boys' responses to the question: "If you woke up tomorrow and discovered that you were the other gender, how would your life be different?" Most boys stated that they would suicide; those hwo did not gave responses of what was bad about being a girl. Girls who wre askded the question, on the other hand, reported the advantages that would accrue to them due to the change; even so girls stated that they would rather remain girls.

[6] In the SASB model this behavior would appear on the Introject surface. We will return to this later in this chapter in the section, Identifying the Interpersonal Sequences of the Shame Event.

[7] Nathanson appears to have made the same mistake that is seen in Freud's work and recent theorizing about women by women: conflation of sex and gender. Nathanson uncritically assumes that sexual experience, especially sexual connection is the prototypical human connection. Sexual intercourse does not equal human relatedness, and it cannot. It is one meager analogy for profound intimacy which involves individuals in an experience of intense knowing one another that may or may not include any physical

touch. However, it almost always involves intense eye contact and the experience of seeing and of hearing and of being seen and being heard.

[8]See Chapter 5 for further discussion.

[9]See Lansky (1992) for further discussion of this issue.

[10]Selvini-Palazzoli, Cecchin, Prata, and Boscolo (1978) have described the schizophrenogenic nature of such cultural prescriptions:
"It's not that you should *do* something different: you should be something different. Only in this way can you help me to be what I am not; but what I could be if you were not as you are" (p. 36).

[11]This raises theological issues about language for God which are outside the range of this discussion. For further discussion, see Achtemeier (1992) and Brock (1991).

Chapter 5. Power and Gender

[1]Interpersonal behavior that serves to avoid shame could be described according to Mowrer's (1961) Two-Factor Learning model, which he developed in order to understand the difficulty encountered clinically when attempting to extinguish avoidance behavior. In the case of shame, pleasure is the unconditioned stimulus which becomes associated with belittling attack (the conditioned stimulus) which evokes shame (the conditioned response). Shame becomes the discriminant stimulus which induces hiding or silence (the operant conditioner) that serves to reduce the shame feelings causing emotional and physiological discomfort. An individual who grows in an intensely and continuously shame-evoking environment might be especially likely to develop a generally avoidant style of relating, Avoidant Personality Disorder (APD). Although I have never seen this shame description of APD, Benjamin (1993) makes an allusion to shame in her description of APD.

[2]Elaborating the mechanisms of this early association of shame with personal ontology may inform theological reflection on the nature of original sin in a helpful way. However, exploration of this idea is beyond the scope of this study.

[3]Some theologians, studying language used for God, argue that male language in reference to God, including the term "father", provides a necessary corrective to human experiences of absent or deficiuent human fathering (Charry, 1993). In relation to language about human beings, Pannikar (19) suggests maintaining the traditional use of male language such as "Mankind" and masculine pronouns, but emphasizes the need for

increased attention to and valuing of the "feminine" attitude of "receptivity in human relations, especially as a corrective for violence and arch militarism in world politics.

Conclusion

[1] The use of masculine pronouns for the child are deliberate here because these theories are based on men's and boy's experience; it was assumed both that girls' experience was the same *and* that girls' experience *should* be the same.

[2] Another approach to resolving this difficulty is to discontinue the practice of identifying nonbiological aspects of personhood with the terms "feminine" and "masculine" altogether. "Masculine" and "feminine" would disappear from the human language, and human traits previously associated with one and not the other would become simply "human." While this possibility is appealing, there is no evidence that the practice of identifying certain traits as "masculine" and others as "feminine" is disappearing. Quite to the contrary, the evidence of the popular press is that men and women seem using the terms with increasing frequency and to be deeply involved in redefining the terms according to new experience. Sociological research of this cursory observation would be an interesting and useful study.

References

Achtemeier, E. (1992, September). Nature, God, and pulpit. *Payton Lectures*. Lectures conducted at Fuller Theological Seminary, Pasadena, CA.

Adler, A. (1910/1956). The masculine protest and neuroses. In H. Ansbacher & R. Ansbacher, *The individual psychology of Alfred Adler* (pp. 44–75). New York, NY: Basic Books.

Ainsworth, M. D. S. (1982). Attachment: Retrospect and prospect. In C. M. Parkes & J. Stevenson-Hinde (Eds.), *The place of attachment in human behavior* (pp. 156–187). New York, NY: Basic Books.

Ainsworth, M. D. S. (1989). Attachment beyond infancy. *American Psychologist, 44,* 709–716.

Alpert, J. (1978). The psychology of women: What should the field be called? *American Psychologist, 33,* 965–968.

American Psychological Association. (1994). *Publication manual of the American Psychological Association* (4th ed.). Washington, DC: Author.

Andersen, H. C. (1942/1989). *The little mermaid.* New York, NY: Harcourt Brace Jovanovich.

Angyal, A. (1941). *Foundations for a science of personality.* New York, NY: The Commonwealth Fund.

Ansbacher, H. L., & Ansbacher, R. R. (1956). *The individual psychology of Alfred Adler.* New York, NY: Basic Books.

Apter, T. (1990). *Altered loves.* New York, NY: St. Martin's.

Archer, S. (1993). Identity in relational context: A methodological approach. In J. Kroger (Ed.), *Discussions in ego identity* (pp. 75–99). Hillsdale, NJ: Lawrence Erlbaum Associates.

Ardrey, R. (1966). *The territorial imperative.* New York, NY: Atheneum.

Balint, M. (1934/1952). The final goal of psychoanalytic treatment. In M. Balint *Primary love and psychoanalytic technique* (pp. 178–189). London, UK: Hogarth.

Balint, M. (1937/1952). Early developmental stages of the ego. In M. Balint *Primary love and psychoanalytic technique* (pp. 90–108). London, UK: Hogarth.

Balswick, J. (1988). *The inexpressive male*. Lexington, MS: Lexington Books, D. C. Heath.

Barnhart, R. K. (Ed.). (1988). *The Barnhart dictionary of etymology*. New York, NY: The H. W. Wilson.

Bateson, M. C. (1984). *With a daughters eye: A memoir of Margaret Mead and Gregory Bateson*. New York, NY: William Morrow.

Bateson, G., Jackson, D., Hayley, J., & Weakland, J., (1956). Toward a new theory of schizophrenia. *Behavioral Science, 1*, 251-264.

Baumrind, D. (1982). Adolescent sexuality: Comment on Williams and Silka's comments on Baumrind. *American Psychologist, 37*, 1402–1403.

Baumrind, D. (1987). A developmental perspective on adolescent risk-taking behavior in contemporary America. In W. Damon (Ed.), *New directions for child development: Adolescent health and social behavior* (vol. 37, pp. 93–126). San Francisco, CA: Jossey-Bass.

Baumrind, D. (1992). Leading an examined life: The moral dimension of daily conduct. In W. M. Kurtines, M. Axmiter, & J. L. Getwirtz (Eds.), *The role of values in psychology and human development* (pp. 256–280). New York, NY: John Wiley.

Belenky, M. F., Clinchy, B. M., Goldberger, N. R., & Tarule, J. M. (1986). *Women's ways of knowing: The development of self, voice, and mind*. New York, NY: Basic Books.

Bell, D., & Bell, L. (1983). Parental validation and support in the development of adolescent daughters. In H. D. Grotevant & C. R. Cooper (Eds.), *Adolescent development in the family* (pp. 27–42). San Francisco, CA: Jossey-Bass.

Bellah, R., Madsen, R., Sullivan, W., Swindler, A., & Tipton, S. (1985). *Habits of the heart: Individualism and commitment in American life*. Berkeley, CA: University of California Press.

Bem, S. L. (1974). The measurement of psychological androgyny. *Journal of Consulting and Clinical Psychology, 42*, 155–162.

Bem, S. L. (1975). Sex role adaptability: One consequence of psychological androgyny. *Journal of Personality and Social Psychology, 31*, 634–643.

Benjamin, L. S. (1974). Structural analysis of social behavior. *Psychological Review, 81*, 392–425.

Benjamin, L. S. (1979). Structural analysis of differentiation failure. *Psychiatry, 42,* 1–23.

Benjamin, L. S. (1984). Principles of prediction using structural analysis of social behavior. In R. A. Zucker, J. Aronoff, & A. J. Rabin (Eds.), *Personality and the prediction of behavior* (pp. 121–174). New York, NY: Academic.

Benjamin, L. S. (1987a). An interpersonal approach. *Journal of Personality Disorders, 1,* 334–339.

Benjamin, L. S. (1987b). Use of the SASB dimensional model to develop treatment plans for personality disorder. I: Narcissism. *Journal of Personality Disorders, 1,* 43–70.

Benjamin, L. S. (1993). *Interpersonal diagnosis and treatment of personality disorders.* New York, NY: Guilford.

Benjamin, L. S., Foster, S. W., Giat-Roberto, L., & Estroff, S. E., (1986). Breaking the family code: Analyzing videotapes of family interactions by SASB. In L. S. Greenberg & W. M. Pinsof (Eds.), *The psychotherapeutic process: A research handbook* (pp. 391–438). New York, NY: Guilford.

Berger, P. L., & Luckmann, T., (1967). *The social construction of reality: A treatise in the sociology of knowledge.* Garden City, NY: Anchor Books.

Berke, J. H. (1987). Shame and Envy. In D. L. Nathanson (Ed.), *The many faces of shame* (pp. 318–334). New York, NY: Guilford.

Berlin, S., & Johnson, C. G. (1989). Women and autonomy: Using structural analysis of social behavior to find autonomy within connections. *Psychiatry, 52,* 79–95.

Bernstein, E., & Gilligan, C. (1990). Unfairness and not listening. In C. Gilligan, N. P. Lyons, & T. J. Hanmer *Making connections: The relational worlds of adolescent girls at Emma Willard school* (pp. 147–161). Cambridge, MA: Harvard University Press.

Biller, H. B. (1969). Father absence, maternal encouragement, and sex role development in kindergarten-age boys. *Child Development 40,* 539–546.

Blass, R. B., & Blatt, S. J. (1992). Attachment and separateness: A dialectical model of the products and processes of development throughout the life cycle. In *Psychoanalytic Study of the Child* (vol. 47, pp. 189–203).

Blatt, S. J., & Blass, R. B. (1990). Attachment and separateness: A theoretical context for the integration of object relations theory with self psychology. In *Psychoanalytic Study of the Child* (vol. 45, pp. 107–127).

Bly, R. (1990). *Iron John: A book about men.* Menlo Park, CA: Addison-Wesley.

Bondi, R. (1995). *Memories of God: theological reflections on a life.* Nashville, TN: Abingdon.

Bowlby, J. (1969). *Attachment and loss: Vol. 1 Attachment.* New York, NY: Basic Books.

Brazelton, T. (1988). *Toddlers and parents.* New York, NY: Bantam, Doubleday, Dell.

Bregman, L., & Thiermann, S. (1995). *First person mortal: Autobiographical narratives of dying, death, and grief.* Philadelphia, PA: Paragon House.

Brock, R. N. (1991). *Journeys by heart: A christology of erotic power.* New York, NY: Crossroad.

Brod, H. (Ed.). (1987). *The making of masculinities: The new men's studies.* Boston, MA: Allen & Unwin.

Brooks, J. F. (1993, July 15). The darker side of Snow White. *Los Angeles Times*, p. D1.

Broverman, I., Broverman, D., Clarkson, F., Rosenkratz, P., & Vogel, S. (1970). Sex-role stereotypes and clinical judgments of mental health. *Journal of Consulting Psychology, 34,* 1–7.

Broverman, I., Vogel, S., Broverman, D., Clarkson, F., & Rosenkratz, P. (1972). Sex-role stereotypes: A current appraisal. *Journal of Social Issues, 28,* 59–78.

Brown, P. (1988). *The body and society: Men, women and sexual renunciation in early Christianity.* New York, NY: Columbia University Press.

Buber, M. (1947). *I and thou* (Ronald Gregor Smith, Trans.). Edinburgh: T. & T. Clark.

Butler, J. (1990). *Gender trouble: Feminism and the subversion of identity.* New York, NY: Routledge.

Cameron, N., & Magaret, A. (1951). *Behavior pathology.* Boston, MA: Houghton Mifflin.

Campion, J. (Writer and Director), & Chapman, J. (Producer). (1994). *The piano* [Film]. Los Angeles, CA: Miramax Films.

Carson, R. (1969). *Interaction concepts of personality.* Chicago: Aldine.

Charry, E. (1993). Is Christianity Good for Us?" In E. Radner & G. R. Sumner *Reclaiming the Faith: Essays on Orthodoxy in the Episcopal Church and the Baltimore Declaration* [pp. 225-246]. Grand Rapids, MI: William B. Eerdmans.

Chesler, P. (1972). *Women and madness.* New York, NY: Avon.

Chesler, P. (1978). *About men.* New York, NY: Simon and Schuster.

Chesler, P. (1994). *Patriarchy: Notes of an expert witness.* Monroe, ME: Common Courage.

Chodorow, N. (1974). Family structure and feminine personality. In M. Z. Rosaldo & L. Lamphere (Eds.), *Woman, culture and society* (pp. 43-66). Stanford, CA: Stanford University Press.

Chodorow, N. (1978). *The reproduction of mothering: Psychoanalysis and the sociology of gender.* Berkeley, CA: University of California Press.

Clark, E. (1989). *Women in the early church.* Downers Grove, IL: Intervarsity.

Cook, A. S., & Dworkin, D. S. (1992). *Helping the bereaved: Therapeutic interventions for children, adolescents, and adults.* New York, NY: Basic Books.

Cooper, C. R., Grotevant, H. D., & Condon, S. M. (1983). Individuality and connectedness in the family as a context for adolescent identity formation and role-taking skill. In H. D. Grotevant & C. R. Cooper (Eds.), *Adolescent development in the family* (pp. 43–60). San Francisco: Jossey-Bass.

Corbett, E. P. J. (1971). *Classical rhetoric for the modern student.* New York, NY: Oxford University Press.

Cowan, R. S. (1989). *More work for mother: The ironies of household technology from the open hearth to the microwave.* London, UK: Free Association Books.

Csiksazentmihalyi, M. (1989, May 28). More ways than one to be good. *New York Times Book Review,* p. 6.

Culianu, I. P. (1987). Gnosticism from the middle ages to the present. In M. Eliade (Ed.), *The encyclopedia of religion* (pp. 574–578). New York, NY: Macmillan.

Cushman, P. (1990). Why the self is empty: Toward a historically situated psychology. *American Psychologist, 45,* 599–611.

Dalbey, G. (1988). *Healing the masculine soul: An affirming message for men and the women who love them.* Waco, TX: Word Books.

D'Antonio, M. (1994, December 4). The trouble with boys. *Los Angeles Times Magazine*, pp. 16–22.

de Beaumont (1780/1992). *Beauty and the beast* (N. Willard, Ed.). San Diego, CA: Harcourt, Brace, Janovich.

de Beauvoir, S. (1952). *The second sex*. New York, NY: Vintage Books.

de Forest, I. (1954). *The leaven of love: A development of the psychoanalytic theory and technique of Sandor Ferenczi*. New York, NY: Harper.

Delgado, D. (1989). *Interpersonal complementarity: A study of the predictive validity of the structural analysis of social behavior*. Unpublished dissertation, Fuller Theological Seminary, Pasadena, CA.

Deutsch, H. (1945). *The psychology of women*. New York, NY: Grune & Stratton.

Dinnerstein, D. (1976). *The mermaid and the minotaur: Sexual arrangements and human malaise*. New York, NY: Harper & Row.

Disney, W. (Director & Producer). (1937/1993). *Snow White* [Film]. Burbank, CA: Disney Studios.

Doyle, J. A., & Paludi, M. A. (1985). *Sex and gender: The human experience*. Dubuque, IA: William C. Brown.

Dunfee, S. N. (1982). The sin of hiding: A feminist critique of Reinhold Niebuhr's account of the sin of pride. *Soundings, 65*, 316–327.

Durant, W. (1926). *The story of philosophy*. New York, NY: Washington Square.

Edwards, D. (1991). Categories of talking: On the cognitive and discursive basis of categorization. *Theory and Society, 1*, 515–542.

Ellenberger, H. (1970). *The discovery of the unconscious: The history and evolution of dynamic psychiatry*. New York, NY: Basic Books.

Elliot, P. (1991). *From mastery to analysis: Theories of gender in psychoanalytic feminism*. Ithaca, NY: Cornell University Press.

Erikson, E. H. (1950). *Childhood and society*. New York, NY: W. W. Norton.

Erikson, E. H. (1964). *Insight and responsibility*. New York, NY: W. W. Norton.

Erikson, E. H. (1968). *Identity: Youth and crisis*. New York, NY: W. W. Norton.

Eurich-Rascoe, B. L. (1988). *Empirical studies of the father-daughter relationship: A literature review, 1974–1988*. Presentation at Fuller Theological Seminary, Pasadena, CA.

Eurich-Rascoe, B. L. (1990a). *The Phantom of the opera: A contemporary narrative of women's development of self.* Unpublished manuscript, Fuller Theological Seminary, Pasadena, CA.

Eurich-Rascoe, B. L. (1990b). *The Phantom of the opera: A critique of his hypnotic method.* Unpublished manuscript, Fuller Theological Seminary, Pasadena, CA.

Fairburn, W. (1952). *Psychoanalytic studies of personality.* London, UK: Tavistock.

Faludi, S. (1991). *Backlash: The undeclared war against American women.* New York, NY: Anchor Books.

Farrell, W. (1975). *The liberated male.* New York, NY: Bantam Books.

Farrell, W. (1988). *Why men are the way they are: The male-female dynamic.* New York, NY: Berkeley Books.

Feldman, E. (Producer), & Summers, S. (Director). (1995). *Jungle book* [Film]. Burbank, CA: Walt Disney.

Fine-Thomas, W. R. (1993). *Ontic gender guilt and sexual identity in women.* Unpublished doctoral dissertation, Fuller Theological Seminary, Pasadena, CA.

Flugel, J. C. (1933). *A hundred years of psychology: 1833–1933.* Andover, UK: Duckworth.

For teens, Fox says murder is not taboo. (1995, April 4). *USA Today*, p. A1.

von Franz, M. (1972). *Problems of the feminine in fairytales.* Dallas, TX: Spring Publications.

Freedman, M. B., Leary, T. F., Ossorio, A. G., & Coffey, H. S., (1951). The interpersonal dimension of personality. *Journal of Personality 20*, 143–161.

French, M. (1985). *Beyond power: Women, men and morals.* New York, NY: Ballantine Books.

Freud, A. (1945). *The ego and the mechanisms of defense.* In James Strachey (Ed.), *The standard edition of the complete psychological works of sigmund freud.* Sigmund Freud Copyrights Ltd., The Institute of Psychoanalyses and the Hogarth Press. London, UK: Hogarth.

Freud, S. (1905). Three essays on the theory of sexuality (Vol. VII). In James Strachey (Ed.), *The standard edition of the complete psychological works of sigmund freud.* Sigmund Freud Copyrights Ltd., The Institute of Psychoanalyses and the Hogarth Press. London, UK: Hogarth.

Freud, S. (1908). Civilized sexual morality and modern nervous illness (Vol. IX). In James Strachey (Ed.), *The standard edition of the complete psychological works of sigmund freud.* Sigmund Freud Copyrights Ltd., The Institute of Psychoanalyses and the Hogarth Press. London, UK: Hogarth.

Freud, S. (1914). On narcissism: An introduction (Vol. XIV). In James Strachey (Ed.), *The standard edition of the complete psychological works of sigmund freud.* Sigmund Freud Copyrights Ltd., The Institute of Psychoanalyses and the Hogarth Press. London, UK: Hogarth.

Freud, S. (1925). Some psychical consequences of the anatomical distinction between the sexes (Vol. XIX). In James Strachey (Ed.), *The standard edition of the complete psychological works of sigmund freud.* Sigmund Freud Copyrights Ltd., The Institute of Psychoanalyses and the Hogarth Press. London, UK: Hogarth.

Freud, S. (1926). The question of lay analysis (Vol. XX). In James Strachey (Ed.), *The standard edition of the complete psychological works of sigmund freud.* Sigmund Freud Copyrights Ltd., The Institute of Psychoanalyses and the Hogarth Press. London, UK: Hogarth.

Freud, S. (1931). Female sexuality (Vol. XXI). In James Strachey (Ed.), *The standard edition of the complete psychological works of sigmund freud.* Sigmund Freud Copyrights Ltd., The Institute of Psychoanalyses and the Hogarth Press. London, UK: Hogarth.

Freud, S. (1933). New introductory lectures on psycho-analysis (Vol. XXII). In James Strachey (Ed.), *The standard edition of the complete psychological works of sigmund freud.* Sigmund Freud Copyrights Ltd., The Institute of Psychoanalyses and the Hogarth Press. London, UK: Hogarth.

Freud, S. (1924–1950). Collected papers (Vols. 1–5). In James Strachey (Ed.), *The standard edition of the complete psychological works of sigmund freud.* Sigmund Freud Copyrights Ltd., The Institute of Psychoanalyses and the Hogarth Press. London, UK: Hogarth.

Friday, N. (1977). *My mother, myself.* New York, NY: Dell.

Friedan, B. (1963). *The feminine mystique.* New York, NY: Dell.

Friedan, B. (1989). *The second stage.* New York, NY: Summit Books.

Fromm, E. (1973). *The anatomy of human destructiveness.* New York, NY: Rinehart and Winston.

Gilligan, C. (1982). *In a different voice.* Cambridge, MA: Harvard University Press.

Gilligan, C. (1990). Teaching Shakespeare's sister. In C. Gilligan et al., *Making connections: The relational worlds of adolescent girls at Emma Willard School* (pp. 6–29). Cambridge, MA: Harvard University Press.

Gilligan, C. (1982/1994). Introduction. Letter to readers, 1993. In C. Gilligan, *In a different voice* (pp. ix–xvii). Cambridge, MA: Harvard University Press.

Gilligan, C., Lyons, N. P., & Hanmer, T. J. (1990). *Making connections: The relational worlds of adolescent girls at Emma Willard School.* Cambridge, MA: Harvard University Press.

Gilligan C., Ward, J. V., Taylor, J. M., & Bardige, B. (Eds.). (1988). *Mapping the moral domain.* Cambridge, MA: Harvard University Press.

Gilman, D. (1882/1973). *The yellow wallpaper.* New York, NY: Feminist.

Gooch, J., & Noble, D. (1989). *The primitive somatopsychic roots of gender formation and intimacy: Sensuality, symbolism, and passion in the development of the mind.* Unpublished manuscript.

Goodwin, R. M. (1981). Gnosticism. *Encyclopedia Britannica.* Chicago, IL: Encyclopedia Britannica.

Gough, H. (1957). *California psychological inventory.* Palo Alto, CA: Consulting Psychology.

Gray, J. (1992). *Men are from Mars, women are from Venus.* New York, NY: Harper Collins.

Grotevant, H. D., & Cooper, C. R. (1986). Individuation in family relationships. *Human Development, 29,* 82–100.

Guisinger, S., & Blatt, S. J. (1994). Individuality and relatedness: Evolution of a fundamental dialectic. *American Psychologist 49(2),* 104–111.

Guntrip, H. (1957). *Psychotherapy and religion: The constructive inner conflict.* New York, NY: Harper & Brothers.

Guntrip, H. (1989). *Schizoid phenomenon, object relations and the self.* Madison, CT: International Universities.

Haffner, R. J. (1986). *Marriage and mental illness: A sex roles perspective.* New York, NY: Guilford.

Hahn, D. (Producer), & Allers, R. & Minkoff, R. (Directors). (1994). *The lion king* [Film]. Burbank, CA: Walt Disney Company.

Harding, J. (1970). *The way of all women.* New York, NY: Harper Colophon Book.

Hartmann, H. (1958). *Ego psychology and the problem of adaptation.* New York, NY: International Universities.

Hathaway, S. R., & McKinley, J. C. (1967). *Minnesota multiphasic personality inventory.* New York, NY: Psychological Corporation.

Hathaway, S. R., & McKinley, J. C. (1989). *Minnesota Multiphasic Personality Inventory 2.* New York, NY: Psychological Corporation.

Hayley, J. (1963). *Strategies of psychotherapy.* New York, NY: Grune & Stratton.

Hayley, J. (1986). *The power tactics of Jesus Christ and other essays (2nd ed.).* Rockville, MD: Triangle.

Heilbrun, C. (1988). *Writing a woman's life.* New York, NY: Ballantine Books.

Hennig, M., & Jardim, A. (1976). *The managerial woman.* New York, NY: Pocket Books.

Henry, W., Schact, T., & Strupp, H. (1990). Patient and therapist introject, interpersonal process and differential psychotherapy outcome. *Journal of consulting and clinical psychology, 88,* 768–774.

Hetherington, E. M., & Deur, J. L. (1971). The effects of father absence on child development. *Young children, 26,* 233–248.

Hillman, J. (1975). *Re-visioning psychology.* New York, NY: Harper & Row.

Hillman, J. (1979). *Insearch: Psychology and religion.* Irving, TX: Spring.

Hillman, J. (1985). *Anima: An anatomy of a personified notion.* Dallas, TX: Spring.

Hoffman, L. (1981). *Foundations of family therapy: A conceptual framework for systems change.* New York: NY: Basic Books.

Holy Bible, Authorized Version. (1611). Cleveland, OH: The World Publishing Co.

Horney, K. (1967). *Feminine psychology.* New York, NY: W. W. Norton & Co.

Howard, G. S. (1991). Culture tales: A narrative approach to thinking, cross-cultural psychology, and psychotherapy. *American Psychologist, 46,* 187–197.

Hughes, J. (Producer), & Columbus, C. (Director). (1990). *Home alone* [Film]. Los Angeles, CA: Twentieth Century Fox.

Hymowitz, C., & Weissman, M. (1978). *A history of women in America.* New York, NY: Bantam Books.

Jacklin, C. N. (1989). Female and male: Issues of gender. *American Psychologist, 44,* 127–133.

Jewett, P. (1975). *Man as male and female.* Grand Rapids, MI: William B. Eerdmans.

Johnson, M. M. (1986). Fathers and "femininity" in daughters: A review of the research. *Sociology and Social Research, 67,* 1–17.

Johnson, R. A. (1974). *He: Understanding masculine psychology.* San Francisco, CA: Harper & Row.

Johnson, R. A. (1976). *She: Understanding feminine psychology.* San Francisco, CA: Harper & Row.

Johnson, R. A. (1983). *We: Understanding the psychology of romantic love.* San Francisco, CA: Harper & Row.

Johnson, R. A. (1987). *Ecstasy: Understanding the psychology of joy.* San Francisco, CA: Harper & Row.

Johnson, R. A. (1989a). *He: Understanding masculine psychology* (Rev. ed.). San Francisco, CA: Harper & Row.

Johnson, R. A. (1989b). *She: Understanding feminine psychology* (Rev. ed.). San Francisco, CA: Harper & Row.

Johnson, R. A. (1990). *Femininity lost and regained.* San Francisco, CA: Harper & Row.

Johnson, R. A. (1991). *Transformation: Understanding the three levels of masculine consciousness.* San Francisco, CA: Harper San Francisco.

Jordan, J. V., Kaplan, A. G., Miller, J. B., Stiver, I. P., & Surrey, J. L. (1991). *Women's growth in connection: Writings from the Stone Center.* New York, NY: Guilford.

Josselson, R. (1986). The embedded self. In D. K. Lapsley & F. C. Powers, *Self, ego and identity.* San Francisco, CA: Jossey-Bass.

Josselson, R. (1987). *Finding herself: Pathways to identity development in women.* San Francisco, CA: Jossey-Bass.

Josselson, R. (1992). *The space between us: Exploring the dimensions of human relationships.* San Francisco, CA: Jossey-Bass.

Josselson, R., & Lieblich, A. (1993). *The narrative study of lives, Vol. 1.* Thousand Oaks, CA: Sage Publishing.

Jung, C. G. (1931). The structure and dynamics of the psyche. In R. F. C. Hull (Trans.), *The collected works* (Vol. 8). Princeton, NJ: Princeton University Press.

Jung, C. G. (1933/1971). Psychological types. In J. Campbell (Ed.), *The portable Jung* (pp. 178–269). New York, NY: Penguin Books.

Jung, E. (1972). *Animus and anima.* Zurich, Switzerland: Spring Publications.

Kandel, D., & Lesser, G. S. (1969). Parent-adolescent relationships and adolescents' independence in the United States and Denmark. *Journal of Marriage and Family, 31,* 348–58.

Kaplan, L. J. (1991). *Female perversions: The temptations of Emma Bovary.* New York, NY: Anchor Books.

Kaslow, N., Wamboldt, F., Wamboldt, M., & Anderson, R. (1989). The SASB and the suicidal adolescent. *American Journal of Family Therapy, 17,* 195–207.

Keen, S. (1991). *Fire in the belly: On being a man.* New York, NY: Bantam Books.

Kelsey, M., & Kelsey, B. (1986). *The sacrament of sexuality.* Warwick, NJ: Amity House.

Kernberg, D. (1984). *Object relations theory and clinical psychoanalysis.* Northvale, NJ: Jason Aronson.

Kimmel, D. C., & Weiner, I. B. (1985). *Adolescence: A developmental transition.* Hillsdale, NJ: Erlbaum.

Kimmel, M. (1987). The contemporary crisis of masculinity in historical perspective. In H. Brod (Ed.), *The making of masculinities: The new men's studies* (pp. 121–154). Boston, MA: Allen & Unwin.

Kinston, W. (1987). The shame of Narcissism. In D. L. Nathanson (Ed.), *Many faces of shame* (pp. 214–245). New York, NY: Guilford.

Kipnis, A., & Herron, E. (1994). *Gender war, gender peace: The quest for love and justice between men and women.* New York, NY:: William Morrow.

Kivel, P. (1992). *Men's work: How to stop the violence that tears our lives apart.* New York, NY: Ballantine Books.

Klein, M. (1957). *Envy and gratitude: A study of unconscious sources.* London, UK: Tavistock.

Knoppers, A. [1993]. A Critical Theory of Gender Relations. In M. S. Van Leeuwen, A. Knoppers, M. L. Koch, D. J. Schuurman, & H. M. Sterk *After Eden: Facing the Challenge of Gender Reconciliation* [pp. 225-267]. Grand Rapids, MI: William B. Eerdmans.

Kobayashi, J. S. (1989). Depathologizing dependency: Two perspectives. *Psychiatric Annals, 19,* 653–658.

Koestler, A. (1979). *Janus: A summing up.* New York, NY: Vintage Books.

Kohlberg, L. (1958). *The development of modes of thinking and choices in years 10 to 16.* Unpublished doctoral dissertation, University of Chicago.

Kohlberg, L. (1969). Stage and sequence: The cognitive-development approach to socialization. In D. A. Goslin (Ed.), *Handbook of socialization theory and research* (pp. 236–249). Chicago, IL: Rand-McNally.

Kohlberg, L. (1973). Continuities and discontinuities in childhood and adult moral development revisited. In *Collected papers on moral development and moral education*. Moral Education Research Foundation, Harvard University. Cambridge, MA: Harvard University Press.

Kohlberg, L. (1976). Moral stages and moralization: The cognitive-developmental approach. In T. Lickona (Ed.), *Moral development and behavior: Theory, research, and social issues*. New York, NY: Holt, Rinehart, & Winston.

Kohlberg, L. (1981). *The philosophy of moral development*. San Francisco, CA: Harper & Row.

Kohlberg, L., & Kramer, R. (1969). Continuities and discontinuities in child and adult moral development. *Human Development, 12,* 93–120.

Kohut, H. (1971). *The analysis of the self*. New York, NY: International Universities.

Kroger, J. (1993). On the nature of structural transition. In J. Kroger (Ed.), *Discussions of ego identity in the identity formation process* (pp. 205–234). Hillsdale, NJ: Lawrence Erlbaum Associates.

Kroger, J., & Archer S. (1993). Identity formation in late adolescence. In G. Adams, T. Gullotta, & R. Montemayer, *Adolescent sexuality* (Vol. 4, 185–229). Thousand Oaks, CA: Sage.

Kupers, T. A. (1993). *Revisioning men's lives: Gender, intimacy, and power*. New York, NY: Guilford.

Laing, R. D. (1965). Mystification, confusion and conflict. In I. Boszormeniji-Nagy & J. L. Frams (Eds.). *Intensive family therapy: Theoretical and practical aspects* (pp. 343–363). New York, NY: Harper & Row.

Lansky, M. R. (1987). Shame and domestic violence. In D. L. Nathanson (Ed.), *The many faces of shame* (pp. 335–362). New York, NY: Guilford.

Lansky, M. R. (1992). *Fathers who fail: Shame and psychopathology in the family system*. Hillsdale, NJ: Analytic.

Lapsley, D. (1990). Continuity and discontinuity in adolescent social cognitive development. In R. Montmayer, G. Adams, & T. Gullotta, *From childhood to adolescence: A transitional period?* (pp. 183–204). Thousand Oaks, CA: Sage.

Lasch, C. (1978). *The culture of narcissism: American life in an age of diminishing expectations*. New York, NY: W. W. Norton.

Lawrence, R. J. (1989). *The poisoning of Eros: Sexual values in conflict*. New York, NY: Augustine Moore.

Leary, T. (1957). *Interpersonal diagnosis of personality: A functional theory and methodology for personality evaluation*. New York, NY: Ronald.

Lee, D. J. (1993). *Storying ourselves.* Grand Rapids, Michigan: Baker Books House.

Lerman, H. (1986). From Freud to feminist personality theory: Getting here from there. *Psychology of Women Quarterly, 10,* 1–18.

Lerner, H. G. (1985). *The dance of anger: A woman's guide to changing the patterns of intimate relationships.* New York, NY: Harper & Row.

Levinson, D. J. (1978). *The seasons of a man's life.* New York, NY: Ballantine Books.

Levinson, D. J. (1994). *The seasons of a woman's life.* Unpublished manuscript. New Haven, CN: Yale University.

Lewin, K. (1936). *Principles of topological psychology.* New York, NY: McGraw-Hill.

Lewis, H. B. (1971). *Shame and guilt in neurosis.* New York, NY: International Universities.

Lewis, H. B. (1981). *Freud and modern psychology. II: The role of emotions in human behavior.* New York, NY: Plenium.

Limbaugh, R. (1992). *The way things ought to be.* New York, NY: Pocket Star Books.

Lipsyte, R. (1994, September). O. J. Syndrome. *American Health,* 50–51.

Lorenz, K. (1963). *On aggression.* New York, NY: Thomas Y. Crowell.

Lovinger, S. L. (1994, August). *Voice as communication and attachment.* Paper presented at the meeting of the American Psychological Association, Los Angeles, CA.

Luepnitz, D. A. (1988). *The family interpreted: Feminist theory in clinical practice.* New York, NY: Basic Books.

Lynn, D. (1969). *Parents and sex role identification.* Stanford, CA: Stanford University Press.

Maccoby, E. E. (1990). Gender and relationships: A developmental account. *American Psychologist, 45,* 513–520.

Maccoby, E. E., & Jacklin, C. N. (1974). *The psychology of sex differences.* Stanford, CA: Stanford University Press.

Maclean, I. (1980). *The Renaissance notion of woman: A study in the fortunes of scholasticism and medical science in European intellectual life.* Cambridge, UK: Cambridge University Press.

MacMurray, D. (1961). *Persons in relation.* London, UK: Faber & Faber.

Mahler, M. S. (1975). *The psychological birth of the human infant: Symbiosis and individuation.* New York, NY: Basic Books.

Mannheim, K. (1936). *Ideology and utopia.* London, UK: Routledge & Kegan Paul.

McAdams, D. P. (1993). *Stories we live by: Personal myths and the making of the self.* New York, NY: William P. Morrow.

McCluhan, M. (1967). *The medium is the massage.* New York, NY: Bantam Books.

McDougall, W. (1908) *Social psychology.* London, UK: Methuen.

McFague, S. (1982). *Metaphorical theologies: models of God in religious language.* Philadelphia, PA: Fortress.

Mead, G. H. (1964). *George Herbert Mead on social psychology* (A. Strauss, Ed.). Chicago, IL: The University of Chicago.

Mead, M. (1949). *Male and female: A study of the sexes in a changing world.* New York, NY: Morrow Quill Paperbacks.

Merriam-Webster's collegiate dictionary (10th ed.). (1993). Springfield, MA: Merriam-Webster.

Miedzian, M. (1991). *Boys will be boys: Breaking the link between masculinity and violence.* Garden City, NY: Anchor Books.

Miller, A. (1987). *For your own good: Hidden cruelty in child-rearing and the roots of violence.* New York, NY: Farrer, Straus, & Giroux.

Miller, J. B. (1976). *Toward a new psychology of women.* Boston, MA: Beacon.

Minuchin, S., & Fishman, J. (1981). *Family therapy techniques.* Cambridge, MA: Harvard University Press.

Mitchell, J. (1971). *Woman's estate.* New York, NY: Vintage Books.

Mitchell, J. (1974). *Psychoanalysis and feminism: Freud, Reich, Laing and women.* New York, NY: Vintage Books.

Moir, A., & Jessel, D. (1991). *Brain sex.* New York, NY: Carol Publications.

Molloy, J. (1977). *The woman's dress-for-success book.* Chicago, IL: Follett.

Money, J., & Ehrhardt, A. (1972). *Man & woman, boy & girl.* Baltimore, MD: John Hopkins University Press.

Monick, E. (1987). *Phallos: Sacred image of the masculine.* Toronto, ON: Inner City Books.

Monick, E. (1991). *Castration and male rage: The phallic wound.* Toronto, ON: Inner City Books.

Morrison, T. (1970). *The bluest eye.* New York, NY: Holt, Rinehart, and Winston.

Morrison, T. (1992). *Playing in the dark: Whiteness and the literary imagination.* New York, NY: Vintage Books.

Morton, N. (1985). *The journey is home.* Boston, MA: Beacon.

Mowrer, O. H. (1961). *The crisis in psychiatry and religion.* Princeton, NJ: D. Van Nostrand.

Murray, D. J. (1983). *A history of Western psychology.* Englewood Cliffs, NJ: Prentice-Hall.

Murray, H. A. (1938). *Explorations in personality.* New York, NY: Oxford University Press.

Musker, J., & Clements, R. (Directors) & Ashman, H., & Musker, J. (Producers). (1990). *The little mermaid* [Film]. Los Angeles, CA: Walt Disney Pictures and Silver Screen Partners IV.

Musker, J., & Clements, R. (Directors & Producers). (1993). *Aladdin* [Film]. Burbank, CA: Walt Disney.

Mussen, P. H., Conger, J., & Kagen, H. (1969). *Child development and personality.* New York, NY: Harper & Row.

Mussen, P. H., & Dikstra, L. (1961). Child-rearing antecedents of masculine identification in kindergarten boys. *Child Development, 31,* 89–100.

Myers, M. F. (1989). *Men and divorce.* New York, NY: Guilford.

Nathanson, D. L., (Ed.). (1987). *The many faces of shame.* New York, NY: Guilford.

Nathanson, D. L. (1992). *Shame and pride: Affect, sex and the birth of the self.* Scranton, PA: W. W. Norton.

Nelson, J. B. (1988). *The intimate connection: Male sexuality, masculine spirituality.* Philadelphia, PA: Westminster.

Office for Sex Equity in Education (1989). *Influence of Gender Role Socialization upon the Perceptions of Children.* Lansing, MI: Michigan Department of Education

Ogden, T. H. (1982). *Projective identification and psychotherapeutic technique.* Northvale, NJ: Jason Aronson.

Ogden, T. H. (1994). *Subjects of analysis.* Northvale, NJ: Jason Aronson.

Okiyama, S. (1989). *The complementarity principle: Interpersonal status as an intervening variable.* Unpublished doctoral dissertation, Fuller Theological Seminary, Pasadena, CA.

Onions, C. T., Friedrichson, G. W. S., & Burchfield, R. W. (Eds.). (1976). *The Oxford dictionary of English etymology.* Oxford: Clarendon.

Pagels, E. (1979). *The gnostic gospels.* New York, NY: Vintage Books.

Pagels, E. (1988). *Adam, Eve and the serpent.* New York, NY: Vintage Books.

Paglia, C. (1990, March). Feminism and the forgotten power of sex. *Harper's Magazine*, 32–38.

Panniker, Raimon (19). *Cultural Disarmament.*

Perkins, P. (1987). Gnosticism as Christian Heresy. In M. Eliade (Ed.), *The encyclopedia of religion* (pp. 578–580). New York, NY: Macmillan.

Perry, W. G. (1970). *Forms of intellectual and ethical development in the college years.* New York, NY: Holt, Rinehart, & Winston.

Phares, V. (1992). Where's Poppa? The relative lack of attention to the role of fathers in child and adolescent psychopathology. *American Psychologist, 47(5)*, 656–664.

Pleck, J. H. (1981). *The myth of masculinity.* Cambridge, MA: MIT.

Popper, K. (1957). *The poverty of historicism.* New York: Harper & Row.

Promisekeepers. (1994). *Seven promises of a promisekeeper.* Colorado Springs, CO: Focus on the Family.

Qualls-Corbett, N. (1988). *The sacred prostitute: Eternal aspect of the feminine.* Toronto, Canada: Inner City Books.

Quispel, G. (1987). Gnosticism from its origins to the middle ages. In M. Eliade (Ed.), *The encyclopedia of religion* (pp. 566–574). New York, NY: Macmillan.

Ranke-Heinemann, U. (1990). *Eunuchs for the kingdom of heaven: Women, sexuality, and the Catholic Church.* Garden City, NY: Doubleday.

Rausch, H. (1965). Interaction sequences. *Journal of Personality and Social Psychology, 2*, 487–499.

Reis, D., Olevinci, M. E., & Curd, K. (1983). Family paradigm and adolescent social behavior. In H. D. Grotevant & C. R. Cooper, (Eds.) *Adolescent development in the family* (pp. 77–92). San Francisco, CA: Jossey-Basse.

Riger, S. (1992). Epistemological debates, feminist voices: Science, social values, and the study of women. *American Psychologist, 47(6)*, 730–740.

Rotzien, M. K. (1989). *A critique of the double bind system: Theory, methodology, and research.* Unpublished doctoral dissertation, Fuller Theological Seminary, Pasadena, CA.

Rotzien, M. K., & Vande Kemp, H. (1989a). *A brief report on the double-bind system and SASB methodology: suggestions for research.* Unpublished manuscript, Fuller Theological Seminary, Pasadena, CA.

Rotzien, M. K., & Vande Kemp, H. (1989b). *The double-bind system: Advances utilizing coordinated management of meaning and structural analysis of social behavior.* Unpublished manuscript, Fuller Theological Seminary, Pasadena, CA.

Sampson, E. E. (1978). Scientific paradigmatic social value: Wanted: a scientific revolution. *Journal of Personality and Social Psychology 36,* 1332–1343.

Sampson, E. E. (1993). Identity Politics: Challenges to psychology and understanding. *American Psychologist, 48,* 1219–1230.

Satir, V. (1967). *Conjoint family therapy.* Palo Alto, CA: Science & Behavior Books.

Schafer, R. (1992). *Retelling a life: Narration and dialogue in psychoanalysis.* New York, NY: Basic Books.

Schneider, A. Z. (1994, August). *Discussion: Overtones of the voice. Gender implications in the therapeutic situation.* Paper presented at the meeting of the American Psychological Association, Los Angeles, CA.

Schneider, D. (1987). The shame of narcissism. In D. L. Nathanson (Ed.). *The many faces of shame* (pp. 194–213). New York, NY: Guilford.

Schreck, G. P. (1991). Personhood and relational life tasks: A model for integrating psychology and theology. In H. Vande Kemp (Ed.), *Family therapy* (pp. 77–107). Grand Rapids, MI: Baker Books.

Sears, R. R., Maccoby, E., & Levin, H. (1957). *Patterns in child rearing.* New York, NY: Harper & Row.

Sebald, H. (1976). *Momism: The silent disease of America.* Chicago, IL: Nelson Hall.

Selvini-Palazzoli, I. Cecchin, G, Prata, G., & Boscolo, L. (1978). *Paradox and counterparadox: A new model in the therapy of the family in schizophrenia transaction.* (E. V. Burt, Trans.). New York, NY: Jason Aronson. (Original work published 1975)

Singer, J. (1972). *Boundaries of the soul: The practice of Jung's psychology.* Garden City, NY: Doubleday.

Singer, J. (1976). *Androgyny: Toward a new theory of sexuality.* Garden City, NY, NY: Anchor Books.

Smith, L. (1995, March 15). A dad's role in lifelong success? Significant. *Los Angeles Times,* p. E1.

Snarey, J. (1994). *How fathers care for the next generation.* Cambridge, MA: Harvard University Press.

Spelman, E. V. (1988). *Inessential woman: Problems of exclusion in feminist thought.* Boston: Beacon Press.

Spieler, S. (1986). The gendered self: A lost maternal legacy. In J. L. Albert (Ed.), *Psychoanalysis and women: Contemporary reappraisal* (pp. 35–36). New York, NY: Analytic.

Sprenger, J., & Kraemer, H. (1487/1971). *Malleus maleficarum.* New York, NY: Dover Publications.

Steele, S. (1989, February). The recoloring of campus life: Student racism, academic pluralism and the end of a dream. *Harper's Magazine,* pp. 47–55.

Steele, S. (1990, June). I'm black, you're white, whose innocent: Race and power in an era of blame. *Harper's Magazine,* pp. 45–53.

Steinem, G. (1991). *Revolution from within.* Boston, MA: Little, Brown.

Stern, D. N. (1985). *The interpersonal world of the infant: A view from psychoanalysis and developmental psychology.* New York, NY: Basic Books.

Stevens, G., & Gardner, S. (1994). *Separation anxiety and the dread of abandonment in adult males.* Westport, CN: Praeger.

Stocking, G. W. (1965). On the limits of 'presentism' and 'historicism' in the historiography of the behavioral sciences. *Journal of the History of Behavioral Sciences, 1,* 211–218.

Stolorow, R. D., & Atwood, G. D. (1992). *Contexts of being: The intersubjective foundations of psychological life.* Hillsdale, NJ: Analytic.

Stolorow, R. D., Brandchaft, B., & Atwood, G. D. (1987). *Psychoanalytic treatment: An intersubjective approach.* Hillsdale, NJ: Analytic.

Sullivan, H. S. (1953). *The interpersonal theory of psychiatry.* New York, NY: Norton.

Surrey, J. (1991). The self in relation. In J. V. Jordan et al.'s *Women's growth in connection: Writings of the Stone Center,* (pp. 51–66). New York, NY: Guilford.

Swigart, J. (1991). *The myth of the bad mother: The emotional realities of mothering.* New York, NY: Doubleday.

Tabin, J. K. (1985). *On the way to the self: Ego and early development.* New York, NY: Columbia University Press.

Tabin, J. K. (1994, August). *Developmental issues in the psychoanalytic understanding of the voice.* Paper presented at the meeting of the American Psychological Association, Los Angeles, CA.

Tomkins, S. (1987). Shame. In D. L. Nathanson (Ed.), *The many faces of shame* (pp. 133–161). New York, NY: Guilford.

Torrey, J. (1987). Phases of feminist re-vision of the psychology of personality. *Teaching Psychology, 14,* 155–160.

Tronsdale, G. & Wise, K. (Directors), & Hahn, D. (Producer). (1991). *Beauty and the beast* [Film]. Los Angeles, CA: Walt Disney Pictures & Silver Screen Partners IV.

Ulanov, A. B. (1981). *Receiving woman: Studies in the psychology and theology of the feminine.* Philadelphia, PA: Westminster.

Ulanov, A., & Ulanov, B. (1983). *Cinderella and her sisters: The envied and the envying.* Philadelphia, PA: Westminster.

Ullian, D. (1981). Why boys will be boys: A structural perspective. *American Journal of Orthopsychiatry, 5,* 493–501.

Vande Kemp, H. (1982a). The tension between psychology and theology: An anthropological solution. *Journal of Psychology and Theology, 10,* 205–211.

Vande Kemp, H. (1982b). The tension between psychology and theology: The etymological roots. *Journal of Psychology and Theology, 10,* 105–112.

Vande Kemp, H. (1983). Spirit and soul in no-man's land: Reflections on Haule's "Care of Souls" [Review of the article "Care of Souls"]. *Journal of Psychology and Theology, 12,* 117–122.

Van Lleeuwen, M. S. (1984). *The sorcerer's apprentice.* Grand Rapids, MI: Baker Books.

Vitz, P. (1990). The use of narrative in psychology. *Integration Lectures.* Fuller Theological Seminary, Pasadena, CA.

Wallerstein, J., & Blakaslee, S. (1990). *Second chances: Men, women and children a decade after divorce.* New York, NY: Ticknor & Fields-Ward.

Wallis, C. (1989, December 4). Onward, Women! *Time Magazine, 134,* 80–89.

Ward, J. (1886). Psychology. In *Encyclopaedia Britannica: A dictionary of arts, sciences, and general literature* (9th ed., Vol. XX, pp. 37–85). Edinburgh: Adam & Charles Black.

Watzlawick, P., Beavin, J. H., & Jackson, D. D. (1967). *Pragmatics of human communication: A study of interactional patterns, pathologies, and paradoxes.* New York, NY: W. W. Norton.

Watson, R. I. (1978). *The great psychologists* (4th ed.). Philadelphia, PA: J. B. Lippincott.

Webber, A. L. (Composer) & Hart, C. (Lyricist). (1987). *The phantom of the opera* [CD]. Additional lyrics by Richard Stilgoe. New York, NY: The Really Useful Group.

Webster's new world college dictionary. (1964). Springfield, MS: Author.

Weiss, R. S. (1975). *Marital separation.* New York, NY: Basic Books.

White, K. M., Speisman, J. C., & Costos, D. (1983). Young adults and their parents: Individuation to mutuality. In H. D. Grotevant & C. R. Cooper, (Eds) *Adolescent development in the family* (pp. 61–76). San Francisco, CA: Jossey-Bass.

Winnicott, D. W. (1963). From dependence to independence in the development of the individual. In D. W. Winnicott (Ed.), *Maturational processes and the facilitating environment* (pp. 83–99). New York, NY: International Universities.

Winnicott, D. W. (1971). *Play and reality.* New York, NY: Basic Books.

Wolf, N. (1992). *The beauty myth.* Garden City, NY: Anchor Books.

Woodman, M. (1980). *The owl was a baker's daughter: Obesity, anorexia nervosa, and the repressed feminine.* Toronto, Canada: Inner City Books.

Woodman, M. (1982). *Addiction to perfection: The still unravished bride.* Toronto, Canada: Inner City Books.

Woodman, M. (1985). *The pregnant virgin: A process of psychological transformation.* Toronto, Canada: Inner City Books.

Woodman, M. (1990). *The ravaged bridegroom: Masculinity in women.* Toronto, Canada: Inner City Books.

Wurmser, L. (1987). Shame: The veiled companion of narcissism. In D. L. Nathanson (Ed.), *The many faces of shame* (pp. 64–92). New York, NY: Guilford.

Wyly, J. (1989). *The phallic quest: Priapus and masculine inflation.* Toronto, Canada: Inner City Books.

Yoder, J. D., & Kahn, A. S. (1993). Working toward an inclusive psychology of women. *American Psychologist, 48(7),* 846–850.

Youniss, J. (1983). Social construction of adolescence by adolescents and parents. In H. D. Grotevant & C. R. Cooper (Eds.), *Adolescent development in the family* (pp. 93–110). San Francisco, CA: Jossey-Bass.

Index

Abraham, K. 60
adaptation 14
Adler, A. 62f, 77
adolescence 6, 13, 18f, 71
Ainsworth, M. 22
Anygal, A. 80f
attachment 14, 20f, 67, 81, 117, 119, 138
Balint, M. 22
Baumrind, D. 20, 68, 136
Bem, S. 6, 30f, 40f, 48, 65, 67, 69
Benjamin, L. 43f
Blass, R. 22f, 27, 104, 138
Blatt, S. 22f, 27, 104, 138
Broverman, et al. 10, 69, 97

Chesler, P. 60, 73, 97
Chodorow, N. 11f, 42, 52, 60, 67, 70f, 77, 79, 80, 113, 145, 146

Deutsch, H. 10, 40, 53, 61
Dinnerstein, D. 41f, 52, 77, 146

Ehrhardt, A. 69
Erikson, E. 4,5,10, 11f, 20, 22f, 66f, 138

Farrell, W. 35, 73
female 1, 6, 12f, 16, 27, 55f, 77f, 110f, 121f
feminine, femininity 5f, 16f, 29f, 56f, 76f, 104f, 120f, 137, 139, 140, 141, 142, 143, 148

Ferenczi, S. 63
von Franz, M. 40, 64
Freud, A. 60
Freud, S. 4f, 11, 16f, 40, 53, 58, 59f, 79, 92, 97, 121f, 144, 147
Friedan,B. 26, 40, 41, 42, 52, 66, 68

gender 16f, 27, 28, 29f, 55, 56, 63f, 70, 71f, 77, 90, 92, 97, 99, 100, 101, 103, 104, 125f, 135, 138, 139, 140;
and family 112f
and psycho-therapy 115f
genderality 40, 42, 47, 50, 85, 92, 94-101, 104, 116, 118f, 129f
Gilligan, C. 3-6, 9, 11, 13, 17, 18, 19, 20, 27, 35, 40, 60, 67, 68, 71, 73, 77, 137

Harding, E. 142
Hartmann, H. 14-17
Hayley, J. 97, 106, 108
Horney, K. 10, 40, 41, 53, 60, 61, 92

Jacklin, C. 69, 74, 84, 108, 140, 143
Josselson, R. 20, 21, 27, 67, 110, 135
Jung, C. 16, 29, 40, 41, 53, 62, 63-64, 65, 77, 84, 99, 138, 141, 142

Jung, E. 17, 40, 41, 64, 77

Kaplan, L. 9, 52, 60, 61, 79
Kimmel, M. 59, 146
Klein, M. 74, 92
Kohlberg, L. 4, 5, 10, 66-67, 87, 88, 121, 136

Lansky, M. 84, 114, 147
Leary, T. 43, 44, 105
Levinson, D. 37, 79
Lewis, H. B. 52, 85-95, 100, 116

Maccoby, E. 69, 74, 81, 82, 108, 110, 140
Mahler, M. 10, 74, 75, 113, 142
male 4, 16, 18, 29, 30, 31, 34, 39, 41, 42, 53, 55, 56, 61-68, 70-82, 84, 85, 92, 93, 97, 99, 108, 114-128, 137, 139, 140, 141, 143, 146, 148
 vis-a-vis female 10-13
masculine, masculinity 24, 27-32, 35, 41-42, 47, 49, 50, 53, 61, 62, 64, 69, 70, 72, 73, 75, 76, 80, 81, 83, 96, 97, 99, 102, 104, 110, 111, 112, 114, 115, 118, 119, 120, 122, 123, 124, 125, 126, 129, 130, 131, 121
 and shame 83-85, 92
Mead, M. 40, 41, 66, 142, 145
Miedzian, M. 73, 108
Miller, J. B. 9, 10, 11, 13, 19, 26, 67
Mitchell, J. 59, 60
Money, J. 69
Monick, E. 5, 40, 41, 83
Mowrer, O. H. 148

Nathanson, D. 52, 100, 103, 113, 147
 envy 92-95
 sex,pride & shame 90-91
 and shame 84-89
Nelson, J. 73

Ogden, T. 143

Perry, W. 3
Pleck, J. 5, 59, 74, 76, 108
 projective identification 52-53, 98-99, 101, 128, 143, 144

Structural Analysis of Human Behavior (SASB) 43, 44, 45, 46, 94, 112, 117, 131, 142, 147
 and gender 47-51
 and power 105-107
Sampson, E. 1, 3, 17, 18, 78, 102, 104, 112, 115
sex 2, 16, 17, 24, 28, 30, 37, 38, 39, 40, 42, 43, 53
 and gender 30-35
 and SASB 47-50
 history of 55f
sexuality 16, 21, 27, 29, 37, 41, 47, 77, 104, 106, 108, 112-113, 114, 116f, 122f, 138, 141, 142, 143, 144, 145, 146, 147
 and essentialism 139
 and shame 90-101
 history of 55f, 78f

Tomkins, S. 88, 89, 94

Watzlawick, P. 110, 137